A NATION UNDER WRATH

A Nation Under Wrath

Studies in Isaiah 5

D. Martyn Lloyd-Jones

KINGSWAY PUBLICATIONS
EASTBOURNE

ISBN 0 85476 720 7

Co-published in South Africa with
SCB Publishers
Cornelis Struik House, 80 McKenzie Street
Cape Town 8001, South Africa.
Reg no 04/02203/06

Designed and produced by Bookprint Creative Services
P. O. Box 827, BN21 3YJ, England for
KINGSWAY PUBLICATIONS LTD
Lottbridge Drove, Eastbourne, East Sussex BN23 6NT.
Printed in Great Britain.

Contents

*These sermons were first preached
by Dr Martyn Lloyd-Jones at
Westminster Chapel between
January and March 1964.*

1

The Vineyard

Now will I sing to my wellbeloved a song of my beloved touching his vineyard. My wellbeloved hath a vineyard in a very fruitful hill: and he fenced it, and gathered out the stones thereof, and planted it with the choicest vine, and built a tower in the midst of it, and also made a winepress therein: and he looked that it should bring forth grapes, and it brought forth wild grapes. And now, O inhabitants of Jerusalem, and men of Judah, judge, I pray you, betwixt me and my vineyard. What could have been done more to my vineyard, that I have not done in it? wherefore, when I looked that it should bring forth grapes, brought it forth wild grapes? And now go to; I will tell you what I will do to my vineyard: I will take away the hedge thereof, and it shall be eaten up; and break down the wall thereof, and it shall be trodden down: and I will lay it waste: it shall not be pruned, nor digged; but there shall come up briers and thorns: I will also command the clouds that they rain no rain upon it. For the vineyard of the LORD of hosts is the house of Israel, and the men of Judah his pleasant plant: and he looked for judgment, but behold oppression; for righteousness, but behold a cry (Isaiah 5:1–7).

Those words, as the prophet himself tells us, are a poem or a song concerning the whole state and condition of the

Children of Israel in the days when God raised up the prophet Isaiah to address them. Now the prophets were very practical men. We must not think of them as just literary men or as poets who decided to go in for such a career because they enjoyed doing that kind of thing. No, these men all tell us that they were called by God to deliver a message to their own fellow-countrymen. They did not want to do that; some of them, indeed, tell us quite honestly that they strongly objected to God's call. They knew that their message would not be popular and they did not want to be unpopular, they did not want to suffer.

However, they were conscious of the call of God, and, further, they were conscious that God had given them a message. It was not that they had looked at the world and had come to certain conclusions, as people today may write newspaper articles or books when they see things and put forward suggestions that they think might be of value. That was not the position of the prophets. They say in their writings that everything was given to them by God. God opened their eyes, gave them an understanding, called them and commanded them to deliver this message, which was from him to the people.

And that is exactly what Isaiah did. He addressed his nation and told them exactly why things were as they were, because when he was writing the people were already in trouble. The nation, which had been great and mighty, was beginning to fall on evil days; things were going wrong, and, of course, there were all sorts of people rushing forward to give their opinions. So through this man came this message from God, and he said, 'This is the cause of your trouble; this is exactly why these things are happening to you.' Further, he prophesied what would yet happen to them if they continued as they were and refused to repent and turn back to God.

That is a summary of the message of this great prophet Isaiah, but, of course, it is equally true of all the other prophets. They all had the same message to deliver; they all had received it from God. They gave it in different ways because God did not use them as mere machines; the personality of the man comes through. But the message was God's, not the man's.

But – and this is the point I want to put to you now – here, in all these great prophetic messages, we have at the same time a summary of what God is saying to all men and women. The nation of Israel is but a kind of specimen, a type, which God set forth in order that through her he might speak to the whole of mankind. Now it appeared in the Old Testament times that only the Children of Israel were God's people, but, of course, the whole world belonged to God then, as it does now. They were only his people in a very special sense, as Christian people or the Church are God's people in a special sense today. But the whole world belongs to God. So when we study what God said to the prophet of this particular nation, we are seeing at the same time what God has to say to everyone.

A very wonderful thing that comes out when you read the Bible and get to know it thoroughly is that you find that the Bible is a very contemporary and up-to-date book. It is a book that speaks to every age and generation because mankind remains the same in all its essential qualities, and God remains the same. So the message of God to the world is still this old, old message, and I want to show you how relevant it is to the world today.

Look at these Children of Israel: they were in trouble; things were going wrong, and now at last, after a long time, they were beginning to see it. So what was wrong?

How had this come to pass? What could be done about it? These were the questions. And it is exactly the same today. The whole world is in trouble, everybody must see it. It is a confused, unhappy world. There are problems in general and there are problems which are individual and particular. Nobody goes through this world without realising that there is an element of struggle and difficulty. The newspapers are always holding that before us – the tragedies that take place, the unhappiness, the disappointment.

Now men and women come to see this, but the difficulty is that they are baffled and bewildered as to the cause. And there is no more practical book than the Bible. It is the book that speaks to the world as it is at this very minute. Why are we not all perfectly happy? Why are the nations not embracing one another and working together for good? Why the troubles, the discords, the unhappiness and the consequent pain which is so evident everywhere?

The world is still baffled with respect to that and all sorts of people are giving their opinions. But it is my business and my function to hold before you this word of God – to show you what God says to the world today, exactly as he said it through his servant, the prophet Isaiah, some eight centuries before the birth of Christ. The world today either does not believe in God at all, or, if it does believe, it is fighting against him, blaming him for it all, asking, 'Why does God allow this?' and so on, full of grumbling and complaining. That is the attitude of modern men and women, just as it was the attitude of the Children of Israel in the time of the prophet Isaiah.

Now this is the one great message of the Bible from beginning to end – it gives God's answer to the questions: What is wrong with men and women? Why have they become what they are? How can it all be put right? And the Bible has an endless variety of ways of putting that message before us: in plain open teaching, in history, and then, sometimes, as here in Isaiah 5, in the form of a picture or a poem. Here we see again the great kindness and mercy and compassion of God. We are all different and one presentation of the truth helps one person, while another way of putting it helps another. So the message is put to us in many different ways in order that we may all come to an understanding of the truth.

Let us, then, look at it as we have it in this particular poem. Isaiah, in other parts of his great book, puts the truth bluntly, plainly and clearly. But here he writes a poem, he paints a picture, and it is the picture of a man who made a vineyard for himself. He picked the best place he could find, on a very fruitful hill with fertile ground. He took all the stones out of it, fenced it, put a wall round it and built a tower. Then he planted these choice vines and he was looking for a most wonderful yield.

But, alas, instead of getting a fine crop of the juiciest and sweetest grapes, he found nothing but wild grapes. Isaiah explains here why this happened, and makes a pronouncement as to what this man would do. Then, having painted his picture, having written his poem, Isaiah himself applies it and says, 'For the vineyard of the LORD of hosts is the house of Israel, and the men of Judah his pleasant plant: and he looked for judgment, but behold oppression; for righteousness, but behold a cry' (v. 7).

So, then, let me show you that this poem is a perfect representation of the great message of the Bible with respect to the whole human race. This is the message of the Christian gospel, of God's salvation, to the world today, and there is nothing more urgently relevant than this. Here, in one poem, the prophet has first of all painted for us a great general picture – he will come to details later – in order that we may see what men and women are and why they are like that. Isaiah shows, too, the consequences and the only hope of deliverance and escape.

What is the matter with the world? Why are things as they are? The Bible, from beginning to end, always gives this answer: first, men and women are, ultimately, in trouble because they do not know and will not believe the real truth about themselves. Now that strikes the modern ear, of course, as being almost ridiculous, because our proud boast is that we have greater knowledge than anybody has ever had before us. Foolish people talk about the new knowledge that we have about human nature as the result of Freud's work and so on – all this theorising that has characterised this twentieth century. But the fact of the matter is that the chief trouble of men and women is still that they are appallingly ignorant about themselves.

That was always the main trouble with the Children of Israel. Here was a nation that God had made for himself. There were other nations in the world, but at a given point God took a man called Abram (or Abraham) who lived in Ur of the Chaldees, and called him out. God said, 'I want to speak to you. I want to give you a message. I want to make a nation out of you, a people for myself.' And he did that. So the nation of Israel was unlike every other nation. But her constant trouble arose from the fact that she never realised that truth. She always wanted to think of herself in terms of other nations. She did not like this uniqueness; she did not like the responsibility; she did not like having Ten Commandments and a moral law. She said, 'Why can't we do what everybody else is doing? These other people don't have to observe the Sabbath, they can eat anything they like, they can marry anybody. Why should we always have to be different?' That was their constant trouble. They never realised who they were, and their uniqueness as a nation and as a people. And that remains humanity's main trouble. It is ignorant of the truth about itself. What is that truth? The answer is given in this poem. Men and women are created by God. As this man made this vineyard for himself, so God has made men and women for himself.

Now you can see at a glance that this is a fundamental point. Are men and women only animals? Are they really the result of the operation of some blind force that has been exercising its power in protoplasm and has at last produced human beings? Is there nothing outside them, nothing beyond them? Or are they unique and absolutely special, created by Almighty God for himself and for his own pleasure and enjoyment? Are men and women some sort of biological accident, or are they the crown of God's creation? And the whole case of the Bible, of course, is that the second is the truth.

But let us work out the details which are painted so perfectly in this picture. You notice that what we are told about the vineyard is this: 'He fenced it, and gathered out the stones thereof, and planted it with the choicest vine.' What a wonderful picture of creation this is; of God, as it were, making the world for mankind! The man in the picture took this very fruitful hill and having put it perfectly in order, he 'planted it with the choicest vine'. That is just a picture and a parable of what we are told at the beginning of Genesis about the creation of men and women. 'And God said, Let us make man in our own image, after our likeness . . .' – 'choicest vine'! Man is not merely an animal, whatever you may like to say about the development of that animal. True, man has a body and there is of course a kind of relationship to the animal, but the thing that makes man man is this 'choice' thing about him.

'God breathed into his nostrils the breath of life; and man became a living soul' (Gen 2:7). God put his own nature – the 'choicest vine' – something of himself, into man. Men and women are made 'in the image and the likeness' of God.

I have often said that if I had no other reason for being a Christian and rejecting all the popular theories about humanity, to me this would be enough. All the other ideas are an insult to men and women; they make them something small. But here, look at them; look at their greatness, their uniqueness, made in the image and the likeness of God, with a divine stamp upon them, the image of God upon their soul.

And then let me emphasise this other thing. God placed the man and the woman on what is called in Isaiah 'a very fruitful hill', and, we are told, 'he fenced it, and gathered out the stones thereof'. Now this is a poem and people like pictures, do they not? People say they cannot read or listen to long sermons, but pictures, ah, they can 'get it' from a picture. So I am holding the picture before you. Here is man placed in – where? Paradise! A 'fruitful hill'! Perfect surroundings.

Now it is of the very essence of the biblical case to say that at the beginning this world in which we find ourselves was not as it is now. This is a fallen world. God made man and woman in his own image and he put them into Paradise. This choice vine was planted on a 'very fruitful hill' with the finest soil conceivable, facing a southward aspect, with everything that was favourable and designed to stimulate growth and production. So the man and the woman were made by God and put into a position of perfection in Paradise. Now we are forever trying to understand why the world is as it is, and the answer is that it became this, it was not made like this, it was not meant to be like this. This is wrong, this is the Fall, this is the evil.

And we must notice one of the details here. The picture tells us that he 'built a tower in the midst of it'. What does that mean? Well, the purpose of building a tower in those ancient vineyards was that when the owner of the vineyard was anxious to go there, to have a look round and to enjoy the wonderful crop that was growing, if he felt like staying a night there, then he had the tower, and he could go into it. He could have his meals there, he could sleep there, he could do anything he liked there. He built the tower in the midst of the vineyard for his own convenience. The tower was also used for the purpose of protection and so on, but primarily it was that he might spend some of his time there enjoying it all.

What a perfect picture this is of what we are told about the origin of man. God made man in his own image and put him in Paradise, and he came down and talked to him and communed with him there – man was the companion of God! That is the picture that we are given. The great God had made man and woman for himself not only that they might have companionship with him, but that he might have companionship with them. He made them for his own pleasure and his own glory, and he set them there in the midst of the Garden, in Paradise. And what did he expect of them? Well, it is all here. In the terms of Isaiah's picture, he expected them to 'bring forth grapes'; or, in the application, 'he looked for judgment', which means justice, and he looked for 'righteousness', which means truth and holy living.

Now this is obviously a very vital matter today. One almost cannot pick up a newspaper without reading something about the problem of the so-called 'new morality', so the whole question before the modern world is:

What is morality? How are we meant to live? Some of the fundamental rules for living are being questioned at this present time. Is marriage sacred, something binding, or is it not? Is there loyalty or is there not? And you cannot raise those questions without raising the fundamental question of what men and women are. Are they, after all, animals? Must they be expected to behave as the animals do in the farmyard or the jungle? There is promiscuity in nature, is there not? So is it all right in human beings? Well, if they are only animals, why not?

The answer to all this is found in the biblical answer to the question: What are men and women? And when you realise what they are, you ask your second question: What are they meant to do? How are they meant to live? The answer is quite plain. God, having made them in his own image, obviously expected certain things from them. He made them lords of creation, and therefore he expected them to live differently from the creation. The animals live by their instincts and they obey them. That is all right, they are animals, you would not dream of correcting or chastising an animal because it behaves in an indiscriminate and promiscuous manner, there is nothing wrong in that. But do you expect a man and a woman to live like that? No! He looked for justice; he looked for righteousness; he looked for judgement.

This is the biblical view of men and women; that having been made in the very image and likeness of God they are responsible to God; they are meant to live according to a certain standard; they are meant to honour God's law; they are meant to be the companions of God. That is what God expects of us. He expects us to be righteous, to be disciplined, to be controlled and pure; to reflect something of his glory; to be masters of our faculties instead of being governed by them. That is what God looks for – for

'judgment' and for 'righteousness'. These are just the
ways in which, in this picture, the prophet Isaiah reminds
us of the essential truth concerning human beings, our
origin, our nature, what we are meant to be and how we
are meant to live.

The second general principle that Isaiah lays down is
this: the utter unreasonableness of human behaviour and
conduct. Here it is in this question: 'And now, O inhabitants of Jerusalem, and men of Judah, judge, I pray you,
betwixt me and my vineyard.' In other words, he is making
an appeal to reason, to understanding and to common
sense.

'Look here,' says the owner of the vineyard, 'that is
how I planted my choicest vine on that most fruitful hill.
I gave it every chance and opportunity. I ask you in all
fairness, judge between me and my vineyard. Come
along, constitute yourselves as a jury, give your verdict on
the conduct of this vineyard.'

And that is precisely another great argument of the Bible
– the utter unreasonableness of men and women in their
lives, and their sin. Consider the way in which they have
lived and have behaved, and how they are behaving at this
present time. What is the essential cause of all their ills?
Here it is in a word – disobedience! Rebellion! And I want
to show you the utter unreasonableness of that. Here are
man and woman made in the image of God and placed in
perfect surroundings, given an ideal life of communion
with God, meant to enjoy this life of righteousness and
holiness. What have they done? They have deliberately
flouted God's law; they have rebelled against him; they
have turned their back upon him, and have gone in the
opposite direction.

Now that is unreasonable for this reason: What is wrong
with God's way? What is wrong with what God expects of

men and women? Why is it that people are living without God? Why is it that they think they are clever when they flout God's laws and spit upon the sanctities and ignore the teaching of the Lord Jesus Christ? Why do they do that?

Let me put it like this: How do you justify the godless life? To put it positively: What is wrong with God's demand? 'He looked for judgment . . . he looked for righteousness.' What is wrong with that? Tell me, in the name of reason, what is your objection to the Ten Commandments? Take the first four. Worship God and him alone; do not bow down to graven images. Is there anything wrong in that? Why should people want to bow down to a graven image? 'Thou shalt not take the name of the LORD thy God in vain.' Why should you object to that? 'Remember the sabbath day, to keep it holy.' What is wrong with keeping the Sabbath? Even medical men tell you that it is good for us to take one day of rest in seven. Why should you not cultivate your mind and your spirit and think of eternity – what is the objection?

But let us come to the last six, to the practical Commandments. 'Thou shalt not kill.' What is your objection to that? Is it reasonable to want to kill? 'Thou shalt not steal.' Oh, that is unreasonable, is it? The reasonable thing is to steal, to take other people's belongings and property? 'Honour thy father and mother.' You were born of them into this world and they cared for you; they gave up their nights of rest for you; there was nothing they would not do for you; they showered their love upon you. Is it unreasonable to ask you to honour them?

I put it to you as this man says – 'And now, O inhabitants of Jerusalem, and men of Judah, judge, I pray you, betwixt me and my vineyard.' Where is the unreasonableness of God's demand in the Ten Commandments? 'Thou

shalt not commit adultery.' Is it unreasonable to ask
people to keep their marriage pledge and vow? Is it wrong
to ask them to exercise a little restraint? Is it wrong to ask
a man not to covet another man's wife and not to upset
his family and bring havoc and ruin upon them – is it
unreasonable? Face it! And so with every other demand
that God has ever made. 'He looked for judgment . . . for
righteousness': the Ten Commandments, the moral law,
the Sermon on the Mount. What is wrong with them?

Do you not realise that if everybody in the world were
keeping the Ten Commandments and the Sermon on the
Mount, there would be no danger of war, nobody would
be building armaments and there would be no international tension? And we would not have all the moral
problems we face today, we would not need to set up all
these royal commissions, and there would not be such
havoc in married life and in home life with all the consequent misery and wretchedness.

Oh, mankind is mad. This is insanity. It is the height of
unreason! The rebellion of men and women against God,
and their flouting of his holy law, is the height of irrationality. They are not reasonable animals, they are fools!
They are being governed by their instincts and desires,
not by their minds and brains. Here it is, in Isaiah 5, all in
the form of an ancient picture painted eight hundred years
before the birth of Christ.

Isaiah's third point is the perversion which is so characteristic of human behaviour. He says this twice over: 'He
looked that it should bring forth grapes, and it brought
forth wild grapes . . . . Wherefore, when I looked that it
should bring forth grapes, brought it forth wild grapes?'
And, 'He looked for judgment, but behold oppression;
for righteousness, but behold a cry.' That is perversion.
Men and women were producing the exact opposite of

what they were meant to produce. They were meant to be like a fruitful vine, producing the most luscious, delightful grapes in their sweetness and their succulence, but they were actually producing 'wild grapes'; and wild grapes are not any good, they have no value, no sustenance, they are offensive and bitter. They are useless, a pretence and a sham. They look like the real thing, so you put them in your mouth, only to find that they are not, and you spit them out.

And is that not a perfect summary of the whole of human life? Do you ask me to believe that people were meant to be producing the results they are producing today? Look at the world and tabulate what it is doing: drunkenness, theft, adultery, fornication, violence, jealousy, envy, spite, malice, hatred. It is useless and bitter; it is to be spat out. If people were in their senses they would revile and renounce it. The world is producing nothing that is of ultimate value. It is producing a sham, an appearance of living that is not living; it is existence, and an evil and a finally useless existence. It is all in this picture. 'He looked that it should bring forth grapes, and it brought forth wild grapes' – with all their sourness and bitterness. That is perversion. Men and women are twisted. They were never meant to be like this. They were meant to be upright and clean and holy, producing fruits of righteousness to the glory of God, and what we have is shame, darkness and uncleanness in all the strata of society.

But there is something even worse than that – it is the utter inexcusability of mankind. Listen to this plaintive note: 'What could have been done more to my vineyard, that I have not done in it?' Here is the man who bought that wonderful plot of ground, that fruitful hill, took out the stones, fenced it, protected it, planted the choicest vine in it; and he gets nothing but wild grapes. So he appeals to the reason of all the onlookers. 'Tell me,' he says, 'in all reason, can you convict me of having failed to do anything? Have I not done everything that could be done for its welfare and its well-being? Is there anything more I could have done?' And the answer is: Nothing at all.

Which leads me to say that men and women in sin and in their present shame are utterly inexcusable. What more could God have done for them than he has done? The Bible is the record of what God has done for us; he speaks through this great book to every one of us and he says, 'What more could I have done, that I have not done?' He made human beings perfect; he gave them a perfect environment; he came down and communed with them; he blessed them; he gave them everything they needed. What more could he have given them?

But not only at the beginning, he has continued in the same way. Even when man and woman in their folly rebelled against God and listened to the devil and sinned and fell and brought down chaos upon themselves, God did not blot them out. He did not say, 'Very well, you have done this and I have finished.' Oh no! Even when they rebelled and spat, as it were, into the face of God, God came down and they heard the voice of the Lord God in the Garden in the cool of the evening. He visited them and when he spoke to them he did not merely reprimand them, he gave the man and the woman a most glorious promise. He said, 'Though you have done this, and though you have brought all this down upon your-selves, I nevertheless promise you that the seed of the woman shall bruise the serpent's head' (see Gen 3:15). He promised a way of deliverance and of salvation.

Read the great story of the Old Testament and then go on to the New and this is what you will find. In the Old, you see God's kindness to us in providence. 'He maketh his sun to rise on the evil and on the good, and sendeth rain on the just and on the unjust' (Mt 5:45). God has given us life; he has given us health and strength and he has given us food and clothing. If God were to withdraw his providence, everything would collapse, we should all be starving, we should all be unclothed. God keeps us going, though we are rebels against him. His kindly providence!

He has also gone out of his way to instruct us through his holy law. He is concerned about us even though we have fallen and have been disobedient. And then, the most astounding thing of all, we see God's patience and lovingkindness. He raised up this nation of Israel; through them he has spoken to the whole world and look at his patience with them! They went against him and got into trouble, but when they turned back to him, God received them. Most of us would have blasted them to nothing! But God, against whom they had so rebelled, said, 'I forgive you!' And he showered his love upon them. Then they went away and did it again, and back they came, cringing in repentance, and God again accepted them. He constantly did this. See his longsuffering, his patience, his mercy and his compassion.

Look at it in the case of the whole nation and look at it, too, in the case of some of the great leaders of the nation who went wrong and came back. What more could God have done for the nation of Israel?

And then think of the warnings that he has given us. Men and women in their cleverness are tempted to say, 'But I didn't know, how could I have known? If only I had had some instruction; if only I had had some warning.' No, that is a lie. The Bible is full of warnings. God told the man and the woman before they fell that if they did, they would suffer. They were warned. And God has warned the human race ever since. He has warned them not only in words, but by allowing things to happen to them. What more could God have done?

'What more could have been done?' asks God in this picture. 'God so loved the world, that he gave his only begotten Son' (Jn 3:16). His concern for this world and its people was so great that 'When the fulness of the time was come, God sent forth his Son, made of a woman, made under the law . . .' (Gal 4:4). He sent servants, he sent prophets, he sent instructors. Then he said in effect, 'I am going to do the biggest thing that I can do. I cannot do anything beyond this. I will send my own Son among them.' And he did. The Son of God was born as the baby of Bethlehem. He became man and lived in this world, endured the contradiction of sinners against himself, shared the life of ordinary men and women, and then finally took the load of their sins upon himself. He was smitten for their transgression and gave his life for their deliverance.

God emptied his own heart of love, he sent his only begotten, dearly loved Son, and 'made him to be sin for us, who knew no sin' (2 Cor 5:21). He gave his Son even unto death, the cruel death and shame of the cross, and pointing to that cross he says to the whole world, 'Believe on my Son and I will forgive you all your sins. I will blot them out as a thick cloud. I will reconcile you unto myself and I will give you a new nature, a new start, a new birth. I will put my Holy Spirit into you. I will perfect you and eventually I will receive you unto myself in the glory everlasting. I will do it all for nothing, just believe in my Son.' What more could even God have done? That is his own question. 'What could have been done more to my vineyard, that I have not done in it?' He has done everything.

So men and women are utterly inexcusable. It is no use talking about your weakness, the depths of your sin or the power of evil in the world – I know all about it. But God's salvation is more powerful and you are as you are simply because you do not believe it. You have no excuse.

And so there is only one thing left and that is God's judgement upon rebellious, foolish people, who have not only broken God's holy law but have rejected God's grace and gracious offer of a free salvation. Listen to the terrible words:

> And now go to; I will tell you what I will do to my vineyard: I will take away the hedge thereof, and it shall be eaten up; and break down the wall thereof, and it shall be trodden down: and I will lay it waste: it shall not be pruned, nor digged; but there shall come up briers and thorns: I will also command the clouds that they rain no more upon it.

Let me briefly interpret that. Because the world has rejected God's law and rejected his Son and his free and full salvation, God withholds his blessings. He withholds the clouds that they rain no more upon the earth. Do you expect to be blessed by God when you refuse his laws and reject his offer of love in Christ? If you do, you are mad. The whole world is as it is tonight because God is withholding his blessing. It has no right to it.

But he does not stop at that. He withholds his protection and his restraints. 'I will take away the hedge thereof, and it shall be eaten up; and break down the wall thereof, and it shall be trodden down.' In this world we are surrounded by evil forces and spirits and it is God alone who is more powerful than they are, and can hold them back and protect us. Reject God, and in they come; and they are coming in today. All the enemies of mankind are attacking with a mighty and a terrible power – the forces of evil and sin and uncleanness and suggestiveness and foulness. The restraints of religion have gone, the restraint of the Holy Spirit is withdrawn and the evil forces are coming in as a flood, and our moral muddle is increasing from week to week. God has withheld his protection because men and women said they did not need it.

But God even goes beyond that; he says, 'I will lay it waste.' He will make it a desolation. I interpret this as meaning that God will not allow people to succeed and to be happy in this world while they remain in a state of rebellion. 'There is no peace, saith my God, to the wicked' (Is 57:21). So our modern world with its wealth and sophistication and learning is a living hell. Why? God will not allow it to succeed. He will make a desolation of it. And he is doing it before our eyes.

Life was not meant to be like this; it was meant to be like a glorious vineyard, but what we see are thorns and briers and the horror of it all – the suffering, the pain and the anguish. That is a picture of the modern world. The hymn-writer has put it all in one verse:

> Pride of man and earthly glory
> Sword and crown betray his trust;
> What with care and toil he buildeth,
> Tower and temple, fall to dust.
> *Joachim Neander*

So then, I have taken you through this poem in Isaiah, and we have seen that that is what God is saying to the world. What is the end of all this? Here is the message: there is only one hope for men and women individually and only one hope for them collectively. It is to realise the irrationality and inexcusability of sin, and to go to God in penitence and contrition, to acknowledge and confess it, and say to him, 'I see I am all wrong. I was wrong about myself; I was wrong about others. I see that I have been made by you and am meant for you, and that I cannot live without you. I see that I am a fool, I am mad. God have mercy upon me!' Repentance! Go to him and confess it.

And then go on and say, 'I have heard your question. You have said, "What more could I have done than to send my only begotten Son?" And I reply, O God you could do no more, you have done everything in him! I humble myself before you. I believe in him. I come to you.' And God will be waiting and ready and willing to receive you.

2

Materialism

Woe unto them that join house to house, that lay field to field, till there be no place, that they may be placed alone in the midst of the earth! In mine ears said the LORD of hosts, Of a truth many houses shall be desolate, even great and fair, without inhabitant. Yea, ten acres of vineyard shall yield one bath, and the seed of an homer shall yield an ephah (Isaiah 5:8–10).

We have seen that Isaiah in his fifth chapter delivered a message to his contemporaries, the Children of Israel, in the form of a poem or a picture. He starts by stating the whole case and then he proceeds to take it up in particular and to illustrate what he has already said in general.

His general point is that Israel is a pattern or an example which God set before the whole human race in order to convey his great message that men and women, in their rebellion against God, are ignorant of their own true nature, they are irrational and perverse and, finally, they are utterly without excuse. The only hope for them is to realise all this before it is too late and repent and turn back to God lest his wrath should descend upon them.

There is the great picture, given in a nutshell, as it were. But, having done that, the prophet goes on to give us particular examples and illustrations. Now somebody may very well ask: Are these particulars necessary? Is there any need for us to bother our heads about them? Why did the prophet put them in terms of six 'woes'? Why was he not content with just delivering his general message?

There are many who hold that view. The same objection is raised against a personal gospel. Many people have no objection at all to the gospel, as long as it remains in the realm of general ideas, but the moment it becomes personal, the moment it is applied, the moment it begins to put pressure upon them and to call upon them to do something, they object to it and dislike it.

But people who object in this way should know that they are objecting to the biblical method. The Bible never stops at generalities, it always comes down to the particular, and it does this in order to bring the truth right home to us, and to produce a real conviction.

I could illustrate this to you in many different ways. For example, I remember once hearing a very eloquent statesman delivering a great oration on 'The Sanctity of International Contracts', and the theme was the importance of a bond, of a solemn word. Here was a great principle. Britain was then fighting in the first world war, and fighting for this principle. Yet while the man was able to speak so eloquently on the general principle, he was not being loyal to his own marriage contract. You see, it is all very well to get excited about the sanctity of international contracts and to talk about general ideas but the important question is: Do you really believe in the sanctity of contracts? And the way you discover that is not by discussing general principles and ideas but by examining your own life. It is easy to sit down and say, 'Yes, that is a fine principle,' but are you really in agreement? Are you actually observing contracts – in that case the marriage contract – in your own personal life and conduct? That is one of the reasons for always bringing the general down to the particular. It brings it home to us. We must examine ourselves; and the particular will make us do that.

Secondly, particulars, after all, are but illustrations of the general. They belong to the general, and therefore they are a very good way of illustrating it. Moreover, we do not always see a principle until an illustration is given. 'Ah,' we say, 'now I've got it. I couldn't quite get it as a principle, but now, as you put it in a concrete instance like that, I see exactly what you're talking about.'

But there is a third value in these particulars and this is the one that I am especially interested in as we look at this first illustration and it is this. The particulars, as we have them here, if they do nothing else, show us that, in spite of the passage of the centuries, men and women still remain essentially what they have always been. Now, if I make a general statement like that, somebody may take it up and say, 'That's all very well, but how do you *prove* to us that people are still what they have always been?'

My answer is that I find that some 2,800 years ago the prophet Isaiah picked out six things that were glaringly wrong in the life of his nation, in the life of men and women in sin and cut off from the knowledge of God, and I am afraid that it is going to be all too easy a task for me to show that these are the main problems confronting every nation in the world today. The particulars help us to see, in a way that nothing else can, that sin is still sin, and that human beings are still exactly as they have been through all their known and recorded history. In other words, I am going to show that the characteristics of life then are still the characteristics of life now.

The particulars are put here in the form of these 'woes'. 'Woe unto them,' says the prophet. Why is God concerned? Why is God going to punish the nation of Judah? If you are in any doubt, says the prophet, I will tell you in detail. It is because you are guilty of these various things. These are the particulars that justify the general verdict of wrath and condemnation.

First, then, 'Woe unto them that join house to house, that lay field to field, till there be no place, that they may be placed alone in the midst of the earth! In mine ears said the LORD of hosts, Of a truth many houses shall be desolate, even great and fair, without inhabitant. Yea, ten acres of vineyard shall yield one bath' – your ten acres will only give you something like a thimbleful – 'and the seed of an homer' – instead of giving an abundant crop – 'shall yield an ephah.'

What is the prophet castigating here? Upon what is God pronouncing this first woe? And the answer is materialism or worldliness. In that ancient civilisation, of course, it was largely a matter of houses and fields. That was the kind of life they lived: Israel was mainly an agricultural community. So these points are put in the Old Testament imagery, in terms of houses, fields and animals. But the principle is what matters.

If this does nothing else, it shows us that men and women remain what they have always been, that sin remains what it has always been and that there is no change whatsoever. There is no one so blind as the person who says, 'I don't see what the Old Testament has got to do with me.' Don't you? I hope to show you that it has everything to do with you, because though you are alive now, you are exactly what people were 800 years before the birth of the Lord Jesus Christ. The first problem there was materialism and we still face exactly the same problem today.

Our type of life has changed, of course, and perhaps to most of us it is houses that matter rather than fields, but that is merely a superficial change. We think now in terms of money and what money can buy – possessions, goods, everything that becomes ours as the result of money. And here is the essence of the modern problem. Christianity is at a great discount, people are not interested. Only ten per cent claim any interest, and in half of those it is very doubtful, to say the least. What is the matter with the other ninety to ninety-five per cent? The answer is that exactly as the Children of Israel turned away from God, so men and women have turned away from God in this century and are interested in material possessions.

And, of course, everything in the world fosters materialism. It is encouraged by all the political parties. Of course they do it to buy votes, and they know their constituents very well indeed. They know that the candidate who promises the most is the one who is most likely to get the vote. You do not need to be a profound psychologist to know that. The politicians compete with one another in offering more and more and saying that their offer is better than every other, and they all say the same thing. I convict all of them of encouraging a spirit of materialism, and of being very little interested in principles.

I do not say that we should not have politics; you must govern your country. But, oh that we had politicians concerned with truth and principles, with morality and right living, and not political policies that merely pander to the lusts and the desires of men and women! Something for nothing! The newspapers, too, are perhaps even more guilty of encouraging this attitude. That is why they are one of the worst influences in the world, always giving the impression that the real life is the life of money and possessions – always parading this before us.

You find exactly the same in all the media – television, radio, and all the rest. The whole world is preaching materialism, and is not interested in the spiritual. The world tells us to concentrate on this life; it thinks it is clever when it mocks at 'pie-in-the-sky' attitudes and talks about practical, hard-headed people. But the real trouble is not with the so-called 'unworldly' people; it is that men and women are soft, they do not think, they do not know how to reason.

Let me prove my contention. A 'woe' is pronounced, so let us examine it as it is revealed to us here. Here is the thing about which people boast today, this materialistic outlook. What are its characteristics? The first thing we must note is its smallness. What a little life it is! Fancy identifying life with a number of houses or fields! But that is what people do, and in this way they are expressing their philosophy of life, their view of themselves – that to succeed is to possess more!

There is a great illustration of this in the Bible; you will find it in the twelfth chapter of Luke. Our Lord was preaching one of the most mystical sermons that he ever preached about the relationship of men and women to God. He was talking about time and eternity. He was warning men and women not to deny him but ever to be true to him, and warning them against the blasphemy against the Holy Spirit. Then we read: 'One of the company said unto him' – the moment our Lord stopped, as it were, to take breath, a man blurted out – 'Master, speak to my brother, that he divide the inheritance with me. And he [our Lord] said unto him, Man, who made me a judge or a divider over you?' (vv. 13–14). And then he turned to the whole company and said, 'Take heed, and beware of covetousness: for a man's life consisteth not in the abundance of the things which he possesseth.'

Why did our Lord speak like that? The answer is perfectly obvious. Here is our Lord speaking about ultimate matters, about the highest mysteries and wonders of life and eternity, and here is a man in the congregation looking into the face of the Son of God, but he is really not listening to him at all – why not? Because to him it is not your relationship to God and to heaven, to the soul and the Holy Spirit that matters, but some inheritance! There is a dispute between him and his brother about a bit of ground or about some houses, so the moment our Lord stops, he blurts out his request: 'Speak to my brother, that he divide the inheritance with me.'

Then our Lord says, in effect, 'Do you think that I have come into this world, that I am enduring all that I am enduring, in order to settle some little problem like that of dividing an inheritance, some little dispute about property and money? Man, do you think that I have come from the courts of heaven to do that?'

But that is the view of life which is taken by many people. What makes a person? Well, the size of the house, the amount of money in the bank, the goods and the gadgets. We call them 'status symbols' today, do we not? That is what is supposed to make someone great.

What a conception of life! What a conception of men and women! The thing is so small, so abysmally small! A person's life, being and existence reduced to things that can be bought with money! I say again that if I had no other reason for being a Christian, this is enough for me. That non-Christian view of life makes us such small creatures, it estimates us and judges us in terms of goods and the things that we possess, and knows nothing about our soul, our spirit, and what links us to God and the possibilities of eternity. It knows nothing about these things. It is an insult to human nature.

But not only that, it is also utterly debasing. Our Lord again has put this so perfectly. He goes on to say, 'For where your treasure is, there will your heart be also' (v. 34). It is the same problem – 'What shall we eat, what shall we drink, how shall we be clothed?' He says, Do not be interested in those things: 'For all these things do the nations of the world' – the ungodly – 'seek after.' And they do, of course, and they always have done; that is what makes 'life' to them. So the competition goes on: my dress – the other woman's dress; my house – his house; the fields, the cars and all these other things. And people cannot sleep at night because of the worry, the anxiety, the jealousy and envy, the rivalry and quarrelling. What are men and women? What is life? Status symbols! The number of things that they possess!

Now there is nothing wrong in possessing things, in and of themselves. The Bible is not unreasonable. There are things which are necessary and the Bible does not prohibit them. But when you set your heart on them, when you identify yourself with them, and when you cannot live without them, then you are a slave, says the Bible. People can possess things, but when they are possessed by those things, that is nothing but sheer slavery; it is utterly debasing. Our Lord says about this, 'The life is more than meat, and the body is more than raiment' (Lk 12:23). The life is the thing that matters, the soul. Not the clothing, not the food, not the housing, not the fields, not the possessions.

But look at the horrible element of greed that the prophet emphasises here: 'Woe unto them that join house to house, that lay field to field, till there be no place, that they may be placed alone in the midst of the earth!' That is lust, of course; and it is nothing but lust. And once you get involved in this you will never be satisfied. That is the meaning of lust, it is an 'inordinate affection'. An affection, a desire, is all right, but when it becomes inordinate it is all wrong; it means that you are governed and controlled by it, and you will never have enough. Lust characterised the people in Isaiah's day and the modern world is full of it.

But I must emphasise one particular aspect, and that is its selfishness. 'Woe unto them that join house to house, that lay field to field, till there be no place' – then notice – 'that they may be placed alone in the midst of the earth!' Nobody else to be seen! 'I have bought up all the houses, or at least I have got them somehow, and I have got all the fields. I am alone in the middle of it all and I own so much that I cannot see anybody else, and I am, at last, hoping to get satisfaction for myself.' The utter selfishness of it all! Nobody counts but me, myself!

Read again the story of Naboth's vineyard (1 Kings 21). The king, Ahab, had great numbers of vineyards, and here was a little man who had only got one; his name was Naboth. His vineyard had come down in the family; he was not a great landowner; he just had this one vineyard where his fathers and grandfathers and all his forefathers had worked. The king wanted it because it was near his palace, and he planned to turn it into a garden of herbs. But Naboth quite justifiably was not prepared either to sell it to him or to take anything else for it, as the land had been given to his family by God as their inheritance and share in the promised land. To sell it would have been to disobey God's express command, and so break faith with God (Lev 25:23).

The king, however, could not sleep; he could not eat his food. He was miserable, and he turned his face to the wall like a baby.

And then came his wife, that subtle woman Jezebel,

and she said, 'It's all right. Be a man. Are you not govern-
ing? I will soon get that for you.' Then she brought about
the murder of that innocent, poor man, Naboth, and they
thought all was wonderful. 'Naboth is dead, go and possess your vineyard,' and Ahab went into the vineyard.

But when you read that story, listen to the verdict of
God upon it all. God's judgement was fulfilled literally,
with the terrible end of Ahab the king, and the still more
terrible end of Jezebel, that scheming, vicious woman.

That is the story. But look at the selfishness involved:
Ahab's failure to consider anybody but himself. 'Who is
Naboth? What does it matter about his personal feelings?
What does his family pride count? Nothing counts but
my family pride, *my* bigness! What right has Naboth to
refuse? I will take it!'

And that is the trouble in the world. That was exactly
the trouble, for example, with Hitler. He called it *Lebens-
raum*; this great German nation must have more room to
expand, and Hitler would have been satisfied with nothing less than the world. All the so-called world con-
querors are animated by this selfsame spirit. They think
of nobody but themselves; they want to be alone.

It is not only true of tyrants like that, it is true of the
individual. Is not this one of the main causes of industrial
disputes? Can they always be justified? There was a time
when they were more than justified, when people were
not given a decent living wage. I lived through that period
in the 1930s. I began my ministry immediately after the
General Strike and the six months' coal strike of 1926, and
I saw men and women and children on the verge of starvation. It was a scandal! But that is no longer the case.
Now people who are well paid also come out on strike.
Why? Status symbols again. Though they are being well
paid somebody is being paid more, so why not they?

And so you may risk the whole industrial future of your nation – what does the nation matter? It is *I* who matters, and that is the principle, the spirit, that you have not only among the working classes but also among the employers. It is true on both sides. All are out for themselves. We are all, by nature, defending personal interests and it is all nothing but a manifestation of sheer selfishness. What do other people's feelings matter? What do the feelings of a man's wife and children matter if a man's lust demands to be satisfied? Or what do the feelings of a husband and children matter if a wife's lusts are to be satisfied? Hence the trouble and the heartbreak and the problem of life today. The selfish spirit that comes in is an expression of this godless materialistic outlook upon the whole of life.

But let me come to something more important. We have looked at the prophet's analysis of the problem, but what is the real cause? What leads to this? And the answer is quite simple: 'In mine ears,' proclaims the prophet, 'said the LORD of hosts . . .' (v. 9). The prophet sees how wrong this is; but how does he come to see that it is wrong? Oh, God has whispered into his ear. God has spoken and the prophet has heard. He believes it, he sees it is right, so he passes on the message. But the trouble with the other person is that he forgets God; God is not in all his thoughts. That is the essence of the problem of the modern man and woman and it leads to all their dilemmas and unhappiness. They have forgotten God, that is what is wrong. Many people think that they are putting into practice Christian principles. But that will not help them at all if they have forgotten God. You can take up the Sermon on the Mount as a kind of philosophy and say, 'We must try to persuade both sides of industry to apply that.' It is no good! If people do not remember

, such principles are of no value.

Men and women regard themselves as some sort of autonomous beings. They think they are the centre of life. But the moment they turn their backs on God, they make themselves gods: *they* are the centre of life; *they* are the centre of the universe; *they* are the determiners of their own fate; *they* are their own rulers, and *they* decide what is right and what is wrong. And that is what is happening in the world at the present time.

Now that was man's original sin. As we have seen, he was put into this world, into Paradise, by God. But the devil came and said, 'Has God said?'

'Yes,' said man. 'What right has he to say it? We will turn our backs on God. We will decide!'

And so all troubles entered into the life of humanity. The original sin was the sin of forgetting God. Adam and Eve turned their backs upon him – and hence all the troubles. 'In mine ears said the LORD of hosts' – and this is the message to the world from the Bible and from God.

God is still over all. The world is his and it is still in his hands, and our times are altogether in his hands. These Children of Israel in the book of Isaiah had turned their backs on God, they went on living as if there were no God. But that makes no difference whatsoever to God. God is, and God remains. He is over all, and the world is still his, and he is looking down upon it all and speaking. And what he tells us is that as the world is his, the most important thing for us is to know something about him. For we will never know ourselves until we know something about God. We only know ourselves when we realise that we are made by God, in the image of God.

Furthermore, God has revealed his character. He is holy, he is just and he is righteous. He is a God of equity, a God of fairness. 'God is light, and in him is no darkness at all' (1 Jn 1:5). And as he is the maker and controller of the world, he is the judge of the world. So here is the message for us. Men and women go on living as if there were no God; they insult themselves and their own nature; they debase themselves; they pervert themselves; they make themselves contemptible. And the whole time God is looking down upon them. Not only do men and women get their own troubles, and make their own troubles, God, in his wrath, is looking down upon them. Remember: 'In mine ears said the LORD of hosts' – the Lord of the hosts of heaven; the Lord and Master of all those great angelic beings and powers and principalities; the Lord who is omnipotent and to whose power there is no limit whatsoever; the Lord who is absolute and who reigns and rules over all. 'The Lord reigneth; let the people tremble' (Ps 99:1). That is his message, his announcement. He is the Lord of illimitable power and authority and control. There is nothing that he cannot do.

Furthermore, he has declared his will. God has declared throughout the running centuries that this life of materialism, of smallness and selfishness and greed and lust is abomination in his sight. He said more: 'There is no peace, saith my God, to the wicked.' You will find that statement twice over in this prophecy of Isaiah (in Is 48:22, and 57:21) and I feel that this is a word which this generation needs very much. It does not matter how clever you are, how able, how wealthy; if you are wicked you will not have peace. You can add house to house, and field to field, you can imitate Ahab and Jezebel, but you will get no peace. The Lord has pronounced it from the very beginning.

Then I want to take you a step further. God has not only pronounced all this, he has acted according to his pronouncement, so the world is not only guilty of forgetfulness of God, it is equally guilty of forgetfulness of history. When will we learn from history? Behind us there is the great history of this world, so look at it, examine it and try to learn from it. Though Hegel, the German philosopher, was not a Christian, he said, 'History teaches us that history teaches us nothing.' You would have thought that the two world wars would have taught us something, but they have taught us nothing.

Men and women are ignorant of history, for if they were not, they would be behaving in a very different manner. 'Woe unto them,' saith this Lord of hosts! And that is what he has been saying from the beginning.

The generation of people before the Flood had turned their backs upon God. 'As it was,' our Lord says, 'in the days of Noe . . . . They did eat, they drank, they married wives, they were given in marriage, until the day that Noe entered into the ark, and the flood came, and destroyed them all' (Lk 17:26–27). The whole trouble with the generation before the Flood was just materialism. God did not matter. They had turned their backs upon him; they could live a better life without him. And so instead of worshipping God, and being led by him, they were eating and drinking, marrying and giving in marriage, exactly as they do today. They did not have newspapers then but everybody was talking about it – 'marrying and giving in marriage' – 'This man has gone off with another woman.' The world was full of that sort of thing before the Flood. And God said that this was abomination: 'Every imagination of the thoughts of his [man's] heart was only evil continually' (Gen 6:5), and he said, 'I will destroy man' (Gen 6:7) – and he did! That is history.

Exactly the same was true in Sodom and Gomorrah. I need not keep you, the very name 'Sodom' tells you all about that, does it not? And London is Sodom, and high society and low society are living in Sodom today.

Materialism! The wonderful life! Lot chose it, thinking he was clever in leaving his Uncle Abraham to have the mountain tops for his sheep. The life of the cities of the plain! Society! Civilisation! Wonderful! But God said what he thought about it and he carried out what he said. I have reminded you of the end of this man Ahab, king of Israel, and his wife Jezebel. Her skull was broken and her body was actually eaten by dogs. A horrible end to both the husband and the wife!

This is the great story that is unfolded in the Bible. Great nations arose – Assyria, Babylon – who did not believe in God, who believed in themselves and in their wealth and power. God saw it all and he allowed them to go to a certain point and then he 'blows upon them' and they have gone! Babylon! Greece! Where are they? Egypt! It was once one of the greatest nations in the world, with the most astounding civilisation. Look at it now, and look at it as it has been for centuries. Rome! Where is her greatness? Greece! All these great empires! Every attempt at world domination has always ended in the same way. It is all epitomised perfectly in the man, who, speaking naturally, was such a great man, the Emperor Napoleon. He set out to conquer the world, and where did he end? Confined to a little island in the South Atlantic! How different was the result from the dream, how different the end product from the ambition! No, God has said this and God has done it.

And he is still saying this. God will punish this materialistic age and he is already doing so; he turns it all to desolation.

Men and women say, 'I am going to join house to house, and lay field to field . . . .'

'Of a truth' – tell them this, says God – 'many houses shall be desolate, even great and fair, without inhabitant.'

Your great houses will be ruins; there will be no men and women there; the animals and the ivy will be there; moth and rust will be there. Desolation! And God will do it.

There is an extraordinary statement of all this in Isaiah 45:7: 'I form the light, and create darkness: I make peace, and create evil: I the LORD do all these things.' What does he mean by saying he creates evil? It is not that he creates wrong but that he brings to pass the evil consequences of sin. God says: You gather your fields and your houses, I will turn them into desolation.

When man and woman sinned, God cursed the earth, and, in spite of all their frantic endeavours and brilliant organisation ever since, in all their vaunted civilisations, they cannot get rid of the curse – the thorns and the briers, the moth and the rust! So our Lord says, 'Lay not up for yourself treasures upon earth, where moth and rust doth corrupt, and where thieves break through and steal . . .' (Mt 6:19). That is life in this world! Do what you like, you cannot stop it, the moth, the rust, unobserved, will suddenly be doing their own insidious work, and what you have built up will be made desolate because God has cursed the earth, and manifests his judgement in this way.

Now there are some terrible examples of this at the present time. One of the greatest fears and anxieties of some of the leading scientists in the world is the fear of famine, the fear of starvation. Why? There are two main reasons. One is the phenomenal increase in world population, the number of mouths to be fed. But the other is the lack of food, and this is where the principle that we are considering comes in. One of the greatest causes of trouble will be soil erosion, as we have seen in the dustbowls in the American continent. People went there in the past and found this rich, virgin soil. They wanted to make a fortune, so they took crop after crop out of the soil but they put nothing back in. They thought they could get out all they wanted and that it would last for their lifetime! So they cut down all the trees which were the natural protection and the source of moisture. They got rid of them all. 'The more land the better!' they thought. 'Pull up the trunks, have great farms and wonderful acres. Let's get all we can out of it!' And they did, till there was nothing left but dust – dustbowls.

And so in this wonderful twentieth century when men and women have come into their own, and when scientific knowledge has advanced so far, our greatest problem is likely to be starvation. Is it not ironical? Yes, but it is just a fulfilment of the biblical message. If you get land and add field to field without God, you will find that your wonderful fields will come to this: 'Ten acres of vineyard shall yield one bath' – ridiculous! – 'and the seed of an homer' – instead of multiplying itself almost endlessly – 'shall yield an ephah.' You will sow great quantities but your soil has become so hopeless that it will give you nothing. These things come back, do they not? They do not work out as we think they are going to.

What is the greatest problem in the United States today? Well, it is the colour problem, is it not? But how has the colour problem ever come into being? Why is there a colour problem? Because of slavery! They wanted to make money quickly and you make money quickly by getting men to work with you who are slaves. You buy them for a pittance and then they do their work for nothing. 'Wonderful!' said those men of two hundred years ago, and up to a hundred years ago, during the American Civil War. 'Marvellous! We are getting labour for nothing, and we are going to make great fortunes!'

We have gone full cycle and the problem of the coloured

person is a major problem today. The problem has been created by greed, by avarice, by materialism, by a failure to submit utterly and absolutely to God.

So there is an example of this principle in general, and in terms of countries. But it is equally true of the individual. 'There is no peace, saith my God, to the wicked' (Is 57:21), and if you try to live this materialistic life and banish God from your thoughts, you will find you are never satisfied – never. There will always be somebody who has more; or you will feel that you are not having your rights; or a thief comes in; or moth and rust corrupt, and you will think you are losing things – and you are – and the things you value no longer count, they go out of fashion and you are left penniless. It is like that in life.

But then you come to the end of your life and what have you got? Nothing! 'Naked came I out of my mother's womb, and naked shall I return thither' (Job 1:21). I cannot take these things with me, I am nothing but a soul, after all, but I have neglected myself. 'For what shall it profit a man, if he shall gain the whole world, and lose his own soul?' (Mk 8:36). God will not allow us to have satisfaction in things, for he has made us for himself and we are too big for this. God will not allow us to insult ourselves in this way. God will 'blow' upon it all and it will all become desolation, and at the end we will be left in hopelessness and despair. 'Woe unto them,' said God, the Lord of hosts. And what he says he always and certainly performs. He is doing it before our very eyes today – nationally, internationally, individually.

Is there any hope? Is there any way out? Of course! That is why God sent the prophet. Though this is so true of us, though we are such fools as to make ourselves so small, and to insult ourselves and deface the image of God, he, in his great and glorious love, does not abandon us. His message is not only one of wrath; there is also a message of mercy. He raised these prophets to call the nation to repentance: to think again, to realise what they were doing, and, before it was too late, to turn back to him, to listen to him and to his ways, in order that they might be blessed.

And he does the same with us today. This is his message to this modern, materialistic age that is already beginning to find its flowers withering in its hands, and all its glittering prizes becoming tawdry nothings – this is his message. Do not spend your time thinking about *things*; do not insult yourself by saying that someone's life consists in the abundance of the things that are possessed (cf Lk 12:15); do not become a hunter of status symbols. You are a man, a woman! Do not spend your time asking, 'What shall we eat? or, What shall we drink? or, Wherewithal shall we be clothed?' (Mt 6:31); nor, 'How many houses have we got? How many fields? What sort of car do we run? What is the cut of my coat?' Do not be preoccupied with any of these things that people regard as everything and vital.

Stop! says the Son of God. 'Seek ye first the kingdom of God, and his righteousness' – seek that first – 'and all these [other] things shall be added unto you' (Mt 6:33). You will have enough, and more than enough, to satisfy you while you are in this life; you will have started with your soul, you will be right with God, and you will therefore succeed in time, you will succeed in death, you will succeed throughout the countless ages of eternity.

The Son of God came into this world in order to purchase a great inheritance for us. When he rose again from the dead, having conquered our every enemy, do you know what he did? According to the apostle Peter, he 'hath begotten us again unto a lively hope by the resurrection of

Jesus Christ from the dead, *to an inheritance incorrupt-ible, and undefiled, and that fadeth not away, reserved in heaven . . .*' by God for all who believe in Christ (1 Pet 1:3–4). If your treasure is in this world, when you die you will have nothing left. But if you 'seek first the kingdom of God, and his righteousness' you will have this inheri-tance that is incorruptible, and indestructible. Let the world go mad in a final cataclysm and destroy itself; you know that, 'Your life is hid with Christ in God' (Col 3:3), and your inheritance will never fade away.

3

Pleasure Mania

Woe unto them that rise up early in the morning, that they may follow strong drink; that continue until night, till wine inflame them! And the harp, and the viol, the tabret, and pipe, and wine, are in their feasts: but they regard not the work of the LORD, neither consider the operation of his hands. Therefore my people are gone into captivity, because they have no knowledge: and their honourable men are famished, and their multitude dried up with thirst. Therefore hell hath enlarged herself, and opened her mouth without measure: and their glory, and their multitude, and their pomp, and he that rejoiceth, shall descend into it. And the mean man shall be brought down, and the mighty man shall be humbled, and the eyes of the lofty shall be humbled: but the LORD of hosts shall be exalted in judgment, and God that is holy shall be sanctified in righteousness. Then shall the lambs feed after their manner, and the waste places of the fat ones shall strangers eat (Isaiah 5:11–17).

We are looking here at the second of the 'woes' pronounced by the prophet Isaiah upon his fellow-countrymen, upon his contemporaries, which leads us on to consider the second manifestation of the basic trouble of the human race. Why is God's wrath upon the world today?

Why is the world as it is? Well, the second cause of trouble is almost as great as materialism. All these things belong together. They are different manifestations of the same fundamental problem. The second is what we may describe as 'pleasure mania'; intemperance with regard to pleasure! That is what is dealt with in these verses.

Now here they are set forth particularly in terms of drink – 'strong drink' – and music. But, of course, what the prophet, and the whole message of the Bible, is concerned about is not the particular pleasures but the fact that men and women are guilty of this pleasure mania. It is not always drink, or music – what it is does not matter – what matters is that men and women are drunk on pleasure and live for it.

But, of course, even the details given by the prophet of what was true eight centuries before the birth of Christ are still very largely true of the world today. It is not only drink, but it *is* drink, and increasingly so, and everything that accompanies it. What is one of the popular slogans of the age in which we live? What do people believe in who do not believe in God, and in Christ in the Scriptures? What is the wonderful life that is being offered? Is it not this – 'wine, women and song'? So the description given by the prophet has a curious contemporary ring about it. He also mentions 'feasts'. That is also contemporary. Eating! Feasting! Banqueting! The kind of life that is summarised here in such detail.

Now before we come to the prophet's detailed analysis of this outlook upon life, let us notice two general points which are here on the very surface. You notice that Isaiah goes out of his way to emphasise that this is true of all classes in society. This is a most important point because it is one of the great biblical principles that all men and women are really one and are all guilty of the same sins.

Of course we divide ourselves up into great and small, wealthy and poor, learned and ignorant, Marxist and capitalist and all the rest of it. But that is utterly irrelevant because you get people in all these groups and parties doing exactly the same thing.

Listen to the prophet bringing out this point. He says, 'Their honourable men are famished, and their multitude dried up with thirst.' You can still divide up society like that. The world does it – the few in the upper circles of society and the masses. Listen to it again in verse 14: 'And their glory' – he means by that their great men; the great men of a nation are the glory of that nation – 'And their glory, and their multitude' – again, you have the same division – 'and their pomp, and he that rejoiceth, shall descend into it [into hell].' And again in verse 15 he is very concerned about this. 'The mean man shall be brought down, and the mighty man shall be humbled.' It is true of everybody.

The message of the gospel is for everybody; it does not recognise any divisions or distinctions. 'There is neither Greek nor Jew ... Barbarian, Scythian, bond nor free' (Col 3:11), Conservative, Liberal, Socialist – it does not matter. It does not matter what country you belong to or what the colour of your skin – 'All have sinned' (Rom 3:23)! All are guilty. High, low, mean and mighty.

This is a tremendous point. That is why the person who takes a biblical view of life finds everything else very superficial. Some people say, 'This is what is wanted; the trouble is in those people.' It is always other people! But the trouble is in everybody. It is in all classes, all groups, all men and women. That is why all the rest is so irrelevant – all the different kinds of divisions. The trouble is not all because of the working man, neither is it all because of the employers. The two parties are guilty of precisely the same thing. It does not matter very much whether you drink vodka, whisky or beer, the fact is that you are drinking strong drink. It is as simple as that.

Secondly – and this is astounding, this is what amazed the prophet – they were actually behaving like this in a time of terrible trouble. God had raised up a succession of prophets to address this nation because of their state and condition. They were going wrong politically, militarily, morally, and in every other respect, yet, in spite of what was happening to them, this is how they lived. He puts that very clearly:

> Woe unto them that rise up early in the morning, that they may follow strong drink; that continue until night, till wine inflame them! And the harp, and the viol, the tabret, and pipe, and wine, are in their feasts: but they regard not the work of the LORD, neither consider the operation of his hands.

Now to me that is one of the most amazing things about men and women in sin. Almost every single day on the front page of the popular newspapers you find the very thing the prophet says here. Have you noticed it? On the one hand you get some serious crisis – trouble in some country, perhaps threat of war again, something that may lead to ultimate calamity, something desperately serious – then on the same page in another column something utterly trivial and futile, something childish and almost ridiculous. But it is on the front page! Why? Well, because, in spite of the crisis, in spite of the circumstances, men and women are still interested in pleasure.

Have you noticed that curious lack of a sense of proportion? There is nothing new about it; it was true of the Children of Israel. It is not only Nero who fiddles while Rome is on fire. We had it during the first and the second world wars. Though everything was apparently in jeopardy, men and women still went on with the drink and the dance and all the rest of it. This is the curious thing about people in sin, they are such fools, thinking that they can behave in such a manner, at such a time, in such circumstances and conditions. Does it not amaze you that with the world as it is and with some of the non-Christian scientists telling us that this world is in danger, that such prominence should be given to things which correspond to the description given here of life in Israel eight centuries before the birth of Christ?

That, then, is the essence of the problem, and that is the thing which we must now face and analyse together. So let us look at this 'pleasure mania'. You cannot call it anything else. What are its characteristics? The first thing that is emphasised, of course, is that men and women *live* for pleasure – '. . . that rise up early in the morning, that they may follow strong drink; that continue until night, till wine inflame them!' The characteristic of this outlook is that pleasure becomes the supreme thing in life; it becomes its end and object; it *is* life. Pleasure seeking! A kind of hedonism, pan-hedonism, if you like; it comes before everything else.

Now I put it like that because there is nothing wrong in pleasure. Do not think of Christianity as something which denounces it. To me one of the glories of the Christian message is that it offers us joy, and it gives joy which is real joy. No, the long-faced, sour-looking, miserable individual is not representative of true Christianity. Christians, according to the apostle Peter, can be described in terms of joy. Their relationship to the Lord Jesus Christ is this: 'Whom having not seen, ye love; in whom, though now ye see him not, yet believing, ye rejoice with joy unspeakable and full of glory' (1 Pet 1:8).

Christians, says the apostle Paul, are people who 'glory in tribulations' (Rom 5:3). When everything is going wrong, they still rejoice. There is nothing wrong in happiness and in pleasure. God forbid that anybody should confuse morality and Christianity! Christianity is not a message that calls us, in Milton's words, 'to scorn delights, and live laborious days'. No, it is a message of liberation, freedom, emancipation, 'joy unspeakable and full of glory'.

But that is a very different thing from worshipping pleasure, from living for it. That is very different from saying that pleasure is the ultimate end and object of life and of existence and that it comes before everything else. But that was the trouble with the people in Isaiah's time; and is not this very largely true today?

This is a very serious matter. Do you know what led to 'the decline and fall of the Roman Empire'? It was not foreign armies. I know that it was the Goths and the Vandals and others who actually sacked Rome and conquered the country, but it was not their strength and prowess that led to Rome's fall. It was the internal rot which had weakened Rome. And what was that? Well, that was just pleasure mania. The citizens of Rome spent their time in their baths; they had to have golden baths, and there they lolled with their drink and their music. The selfsame thing! It brought down that mighty empire, and it has brought down many another empire since. Most great empires disintegrate as the result of internal rot.

I wonder whether we are not witnessing something of that at the present time? The attitude of many people towards work is that it is merely a means of providing money to buy pleasure. Where is the craftsman? Where is the real interest and enjoyment in work? No, the attitude has changed right through every class. In the professions people are often there to cut a figure and to make money, rather than because they are really interested in their work and are out to discover something new, to help humanity and to be benefactors. Everything becomes, as I said earlier, a kind of craving for status symbols, and so work becomes just a means of providing people with money to buy more and more pleasure.

Even worse, pleasure has become a business! That is one of the great tragedies of life today. People talk about 'sport', but it is not sport, it is business. Men and women performers are bought and sold as if they were slaves. Even pleasure has become a business and a means of making money, and if they do not gamble at it, people do not enjoy it. They do not seem to enjoy the thing itself, only what can be 'made' out of it. And so, increasingly, everything is set aside for the sake of pleasure; work is stopped mid-week so that some football match can be replayed and everybody must see it. The country does not matter as long as we have our enjoyment.

So you see how contemporary the Scripture is. And this is true not only of nations, it is equally true of individuals. This pleasure mania can so get hold of people that they begin to neglect their work, their professions, even their own reputation. Pleasure becomes such a gripping power that they are mastered by it; they rise up early in the morning that they may follow it and continue until night. The 'good time', this is the thing, not honest toil, not real work, not concern about living a full life.

Then look at the artificiality of this life. The prophet exposes it here, as the Bible exposes it everywhere. It needs to be exposed. The so-called glamorous life is the most superficial, artificial kind of existence conceivable. It cannot be maintained without artificial aids; it is artificially produced, stimulated by drink, by singing and by music of certain types. Men and women who cannot be happy unless they are under the influence of drink must be very miserable. Cannot they be happy as they are by nature? Must they have these artificial stimulants before they can be convivial, before they can have interesting conversations, before they can enjoy themselves together? Apparently not. Nothing so measures the misery of this age in which we live as the way in which it is kept going by artificial stimulants. It is an artificial life.

But let me emphasise another element – the degrading element. Do you notice how this life is maintained? In the main, it depends upon two things. First, 'strong drink'. And what is the other? Well, it is a certain type of music, a kind of rhythmical music produced by 'the harp, and the viol, the tabret, and pipe'.

This again is a most serious thing. This kind of life is only produced, and only becomes possible, at the expense of the higher faculties. People think that alcohol is a stimulant, but turn up any book you like on pharmacology and you will find that alcohol is a pure depressant. What it does is depress the highest centres. People under its influence appear to be brilliant – why? Because they are a little less controlled. That is why, unfortunately, people start drinking. They feel a bit nervous and apprehensive, they feel held in and repressed, so they take to alcohol. It knocks off that element, that best element that produces this nervousness, and so they feel freer. But it is not a stimulus, it is a knocking out of the higher, careful, controlling qualities and faculties of the brain; and so people become more basic. But that is how you live this sort of life, this life resulting from a pleasure mania. You do it by drugging yourself, by taking alcohol or drugs.

But that is not the only way; music does it also. A certain type of music, of course, the rhythmical music, which repeats itself endlessly until you begin to sway with it.

Have you noticed people doing that? The music starts and they begin moving their feet; then they begin to sway their body. That is exactly the same kind of effect as that produced by alcohol. You can get drunk on a kind of music quite as definitely as you can get drunk on alcohol – by rhythmical repetition, and especially with the bodily movements. Your higher centres are knocked out and you gradually get into a kind of intoxicated state. And when you get the two together, the alcohol and the music, you have the kind of life which is described here by the prophet, and which is becoming increasingly the characteristic of life in this country today. It is a life of screaming, of abandon, of madness, of men and women no longer having control and no longer behaving in a decent, human manner. And it is done deliberately. It is organised brilliantly. There are people who batten on to this kind of thing, who make money out of it, and make it popular. And people in general become innocent victims and dupes.

Finally, there is this word 'inflame'. 'Woe unto them that rise up early in the morning, that they may follow strong drink; that continue until night, till wine inflame them!' That is a graphic and poetic way of putting it. What really happens, of course, is first that these higher centres of the brain are knocked out by the alcohol and the music, and then the instincts and the passions, the desires and the lusts, take control, and people are full of fire. They are 'inflamed'. And then you get all the inevitable consequences of that. Men and women become like beasts, controlled by the instincts of the lower part of their bodily nature.

There is this element of degradation, and yet the astounding thing is that mixed with it all is what Isaiah in verse 15 refers to as 'the eyes of the lofty'. People who are guilty of that kind of life still think that they are great and wonderful. They boast that they are not Christians. They boast of that sort of life. Watch it on the television and in other places. They cannot shake hands without a glass in one hand! You always have the drink. This is life, this is *it*: being 'inflamed', being 'let loose', having your fling! And they think it is wonderful. It is a life of joy, they say. There they are, singing to the music, and showing all the effects of strong drink.

Let us leave it at that. Those are the horrible characteristics of life without God.

What are its causes? They are put here very simply in one verse – verse 13. 'Therefore my people are gone into captivity, *because they have no knowledge*.' Isaiah has already mentioned this in verse 12: '. . . but they regard not the work of the LORD, neither consider the operation of his hands.' They live like that because they are ignorant.

'What!' says someone. 'Are you saying that people are not Christians because they are ignorant?'

That is precisely what I am saying. There is no greater masterpiece of the devil than his success in persuading people that it is their great knowledge that makes them reject Christianity. But it is the exact opposite. The devil keeps them in ignorance because as long as they are in ignorance they will do what he tells them. The moment they get light – the gospel is called 'light' – they see through him and leave him.

What are they ignorant of? Let me just note some of the things Isaiah tells us here: 'Therefore my people are gone into captivity, because they have no knowledge.' In other words, they do not know that they are his people. That was the perennial trouble with the Children of Israel. They never realised who they were; they wanted to be like other nations. They said, 'These other nations are fortunate: their gods are much kinder than ours; they are allowed to eat what they like; they can marry whom they like; they can do what they like seven days a week. Our God has given us Ten Commandments and it is intolerable.' They wanted to be like the others, so they turned their backs on God and took up the other gods. They never realised the privilege of being the people of God, a unique people, a people for God's own special possession, a people who were as 'the apple of his eye', as he tells them (Deut 32:10).

And the real trouble in the world today is still due to this – that people do not know the truth about themselves, they lack this knowledge. What are men and women? Are they just money-making machines? Are they animals to have pleasure? Are they here to be drunk and to indulge in sex, and to go mad with rhythmic music? Is that a human being? Can you not see it? Are people meant to behave just as if they were animals in the farmyard? Is *pleasure* the 'chief end' of men and women? Are they really here just to gratify that part of themselves? Is that it?

No, no! The trouble with the world is that it does not know what a human being is. It is ignorant of its own origin, of its nature and of its ultimate destiny in the purpose of God. 'My people!' People glory today in the fact that they are animals. They boast of evolution as if this were a great compliment. They seem to like to think that they are but highly developed apes, that they are reasoning animals and no more. They hate the idea of the soul; they do not believe in God and in eternity. It is all because they are ignorant of their own true greatness.

What else are they ignorant of? Turn to verse 12: '. . . but they regard not the work of the LORD, neither consider the operation of his hands.' What does Isaiah mean by this? He says that they are living as if they knew nothing about the work of the Lord. This, too, is what modern men and women do not think about, because they take so much for granted. They do not realise that God is the giver of every good and every perfect gift. They seem to think that a National Health Service produces health! But God is the giver of health; God is the giver of life and strength and food and clothing. People think that they do it, and they are proud of their inventions and their instruments and so on. But if God were to withhold the sun and the rain, we would all starve.

Men and women do not notice the works of God. They are ignorant, they look only at themselves. They are not aware of God's kindness and mercy and compassion. They do not realise that God 'maketh his sun to rise on the evil and on the good, and sendeth rain on the just and on the unjust' (Mt 5:45). They think they control everything. And they may very well face famine, as we have seen; they may face disaster, because of their ignorance, because they break the rules of God, and violate the laws of nature.

What else do people not observe? Well, they do not observe that God has been operating, not only in providence and creation, but in history also. History! Try to explain the history of this world without God! You cannot. The Bible is the best book of history in the world. It is in its pages that you really begin to understand history. You see that behind all men and kings and princes and statesmen and wars there is the purpose of God – God overruling everything! But they do not believe that. They go on defiantly. But God is there. They get into trouble – why? Because they have forgotten God, 'the works of his hands'.

And then, still more, there is the fact that if only you observe the process of history, you will come to the conclusion that this, after all, is a moral universe. You cannot do what you like in this world. You cannot play fast and loose. You cannot drink strong drink to excess and keep on doing it without having to pay for it. God has established that as a law. 'The way of transgressors is hard' (Prov 13:15). But the transgressor does not believe that. People who start playing with sin never believe that. But it is a fact. If you sin, you will suffer.

And the whole world is suffering. The world is ignorant: 'They regard not the work of the LORD, neither consider the operation of his hands.' It has an idea that if there is a God, then the moment people sin, God will smite them. But that is not what we learn from the history of God in the Bible. In the words of the poet Longfellow, what we learn there is this: 'Though the mills of God grind slowly, yet they grind exceeding small.' Sin always catches up with people. 'Be sure your sin will find you out' (Num 32:23). You may have a long run, but it will come to an end. Why do you not learn? Why do you not observe? Why do you not watch the works of God's hands and see what he has always done?

That leads to the last thing – God's judgements. The tragedy of Israel was that God was already beginning to show judgement; he was beginning to punish them, but they did not see it. What is this judgement? 'The LORD of hosts shall be exalted in judgment, and God that is holy shall be sanctified in righteousness' (v. 16). The cause of the trouble is that men and women do not know that they are in a moral universe and that the King of it all is God, that God is the Judge of the whole world, and will judge it in righteousness. His characteristics are justice, holiness, righteousness and truth. Those are God's standards, and that is how God meant men and women to live – not to serve their lusts and passions and desires, not to live for pleasure, but to seek justice, holiness, righteousness, truth. They were meant to live as human beings, not as animals. They were meant to be a reflection of God. That is why God said, 'Let us make man in our image' (Gen 1:26). He made him lord over creation not in order that he might behave like an animal, but that he might stand out in all the glory of the difference, with a mind and a reason, and a control and an order in his life. And God will judge men and women according to that.

God has revealed this throughout the running centuries. It is all recorded here in the history found in the Bible. It is equally clear in subsequent history, and if ever this were clear it is clear today. The judgement of God is upon this world. I have said it before, and I repeat it now: in my opinion, the two world wars were nothing but the judgement of God upon the world. Round about 1859 – the year Charles Darwin published his famous book *The Origin of Species* – people began to say that at last we could do away with God. 'Man is everything,' they said. 'Man is the centre; God is not necessary. Hurl him into the limbo of forgotten things! Man can live without God and make a perfect world!' They said that the world was advancing; poets sang about it and talked about 'The Parliament of Man, the Federation of the World'. 'Knowledge grows from age to age,' and the twentieth century was going to be the golden century. Men and women in their self-sufficiency did not need God. If ever a century has known the manifestation of the wrath and displeasure of God in his justice, holiness and righteousness upon the sin of mankind, it is the twentieth century. Have you observed this? Are you aware of it? Do you know that God is speaking through all this and calling us to halt ere it be too late?

And that gives me my last heading – the end of all this. To what does it all lead? What is the end of this kind of pleasure mania which I have been analysing? What is God's verdict on it all?

To start with, it is a kind of life that will never satisfy. If you go in for the life of pleasure, you will never have enough – never. If you try to find your pleasure and satisfaction in strong drink, you will always have to take more and more. Start taking drugs and you will become a drug addict; seek your pleasure in any form which means a lack of control, an abandonment of yourself to artificial stimulants, and you will never be satisfied. The godless life has never satisfied anybody. It cannot because men and women are too big for it, too great for it. They are meant for God, and these things cannot satisfy them. Nothing but God can satisfy them. 'Thou hast made us for thyself, and our souls are restless until they find their rest in thee,' as Augustine put it. That is the first thing.

But then living for pleasure always leads to progressive degeneration; it always leads to loss of power, loss of refinement and loss of consideration for others. Life becomes more and more selfish as people live for themselves and in order to get their pleasure. They jettison their fathers, mothers, children, anybody; pleasure is supreme and everything else is abandoned. Oh, what a loss of refinement! What a loss of chastity and of purity and of nobility! The pleasure mania always leads to the loss of all the highest powers and the best and noblest qualities.

But there is something worse awaiting all who live such a life – humiliation. 'The mean man shall be brought down, and the mighty man shall be humbled, and the eyes of the lofty shall be humbled' (v. 15). The Bible is full of it; subsequent history is full of it. Those who live a life of pleasure and turn their backs upon God will be humbled.

The pomp will be ridiculed and reduced to nothing, '. . . and their glory, and their multitude, and their pomp, and he that rejoiceth, shall descend into it [hell]' (v. 14). Look at the world today in its pomp and glory, with all its laughter and rejoicing, and all its apparent happiness, this artificial happiness, this artifice, this unreal thing. But it thinks it is wonderful; 'wine, women and song', the brightness of night life. The great cities – London, Paris and New York – wonderful! Here is life! Is it? It will be humbled; the pomp, the rejoicing and happiness will all come to nothing.

Let me give you the words of our blessed Lord himself, who spoke about this. Take the words recorded in Luke 6:24–25: 'Woe unto you that are rich! for ye have received your consolation.' You who live for riches have had all you are going to get, but you will die one day and you will not be able to take anything with you; you will have nothing. You have had 'your consolation'. 'Woe unto you that are full!' You feasters, you eaters and drinkers; as the psalmist puts it, those wicked 'whose eyes stand out with fatness' (Ps 73:7). 'Woe unto you that are full! for ye shall hunger. Woe unto you that laugh now! for ye shall mourn and weep' (Lk 6:25). We have already seen something of that, have we not?

I remember – and I will never forget it – the first week of the second world war, and the terror and unhappiness of these bright people when war came and bombing was threatened. I shall never forget that Sunday morning, the first Sunday morning after the fall of France on June 17, 1940. I was taking my morning service as usual, when I saw two men in the congregation I had never seen there before. I had known them for years. I knew them as scoffers, as irreligious men. But seeing the possibility of the collapse of everything, they had been humbled and had come to hear the word of God. 'Woe unto you that laugh now!' What fools are men and women in sin! They do not think; they do not realise their ignorance. Their laughter shall be turned into mourning! And the ultimate end of it all is hell.

It is put here in Isaiah in graphic imagery: 'Therefore hell hath enlarged herself, and opened her mouth without measure: and their glory, and their multitude, and their pomp, and he that rejoiceth, shall descend into it' (v. 14). The end of that life! It is not only physical death, it is spiritual death, and it is Hades; it is suffering; it is misery; it is eternal destruction without end. The great and the small, their glory and their multitude, the high and the low, the lofty and all others, down they go together, with all their pomp, to nothing!

> The boast of heraldry, the pomp of power,
> And all that beauty, all that wealth e'er gave,
> Await alike the inevitable hour.
> The paths of glory lead but to the grave.
> *Thomas Gray*

So what hope is there for such people? It is all here. We have simply to do the opposite of what these people did. In other words, we have got to start 'regarding'. 'But they regard not the work of the LORD, neither consider the operation of his hands' (v. 12).

Have you seen the truth of this message? Like the Philippian jailor, do you say, 'What must I do to be saved?' (Acts 16:30). Here is the answer. *Stop!* Begin to 'regard the work of the Lord', begin to 'consider the operation of his hands'. Stop for a moment. Stop this giddy round of pleasure, this silly life in which you have become involved. Stop this existence which is only kept going artificially. Stop for a moment and ask questions, analyse your life, ask where it leads. What has happened to those who have done that in the past? Where does it all end? '*Regard*!' Begin to read the signs of the times. Look at what is happening to your world; see what the possibilities are. And having 'regarded', begin to 'consider' and draw your conclusions.

Isaiah puts it in a wonderful way at the end of the passage. When all these others are cast into hell, 'Then shall the lambs feed after their manner, and the waste places of the fat ones shall strangers eat' (v. 17). What a message! What is the way of escape? It is to become like a lamb. Not to be haughty, not to be the twentieth-century man, proud of his science and his knowledge, standing erect on his feet and defying God and man – no – but to become a 'lamb'. Not the haughty looks of the intellectual, but the humility and the meekness of a little lamb.

In other words, the way of salvation is the way of the Beatitudes uttered by our blessed Lord and Saviour. 'Blessed are the poor in spirit: for theirs is the kingdom of heaven . . . . Blessed are the meek . . . . Blessed are the merciful . . . . Blessed are they which do hunger and thirst' – not after food and strong drink or worldly greatness but 'after righteousness: for they shall be filled' (Mt 5:3–7). They will have real, lasting satisfaction. 'The lambs shall feed after their manner.' When the others have gone the lambs will be feeding in their own folds to their complete satisfaction. They will have the satisfaction of knowing God as their Father, knowing that they have nothing to fear in death and the grave and in the judgement to come, knowing that they are going to enter into a glorious inheritance prepared for them by the Lord Jesus Christ.

4

The Cart Rope

Woe unto them that draw iniquity with cords of vanity, and sin as it were with a cart rope: that say, Let him make speed, and hasten his work, that we may see it: and let the counsel of the Holy One of Israel draw nigh and come, that we may know it! (Isaiah 5:18–19).

We have looked at the first two woes pronounced by Isaiah, and we are now looking at the third. The first was the materialism of which the Children of Israel were guilty, and the second was their pleasure mania. Now we come to the third, put in these two extraordinary and most graphic verses.

We are interested in this not because we are historians, nor because we have a purely antiquarian interest, with sufficient leisure and time to read the history of the Children of Israel as we read the histories of Greece or Rome, nor because reading history is a fascinating and enlightening thing to do. That is not our position at all. We are interested because we are living in a world that is full of difficulties and problems, and because we are in a world that is so strangely similar to the world of the Children of Israel when they were addressed by the prophet Isaiah.

That is my sole reason for calling attention to this passage. Indeed, my fundamental proposition is that ever since the man and the woman rebelled against God and fell, the world has always been in this condition and it always needs the same message. And here we have God's message to this world in which we find ourselves and his message to every one of us as individual people.

What are our problems? Why are we so perpetually in a state of crisis? Week by week it comes. No sooner is one problem settled than another takes its place: always trouble, always discord, always unhappiness. That is true internationally, but it is the same within the nation – life is full of troubles and problems, full of difficulties. And we all know about this in our own personal lives. Were we meant to be like this? Was life meant to be like this? What is the cause of it all? What will it all lead to? What is the ultimate end? Is history, as the first Henry Ford described it, 'Bunk'? Is there no sense or meaning in it? Or can we see a purpose? These are crucial questions.

But then, still more urgently, we want to know whether anything can be done about it all. Is there any hope for us anywhere? Are we still pinning our faith to statesmen? We shall be asked to do so whenever a general election comes. We have so often been asked to do so, have we not? I am not saying a word against politicians – you must have government and you must have politics before you can govern. But I do not think there are many people left in any country who really put their faith in the actions of any man or woman or in any party.

So is there no hope, then? Is there anything that we can do to extricate ourselves out of all this and live a life which is worthy of the name of life? Now it is because these questions are only answered in the Bible, and in particular in this chapter, that I am calling your attention to it.

Or let me put it in an entirely different way. Those of us who are Christians and belong to churches attend what is called a Communion service. We come to a table on which there is broken bread and poured out wine and we partake of both. Why do we do that? We say that, 'We show the Lord's death till he come' (1 Cor 11:26). The Lord Jesus Christ commanded his followers to do that. 'This do,' he said, 'in remembrance of me.' But wait a minute – who was he? What is it all about? Why should we remember him? Why should we call to mind his death upon the cross?

The answer to that is that this 'Jesus of Nazareth' is the eternal Son of God. The Bible's declaration is that God sent his only Son into this world, that that eternal person humbled himself and took on human nature and lived life as a man and died a cruel death upon a cross on a hill called Calvary. But why should we remember it? Why did he come from heaven to earth and go to that death? His disciples tried to stop him; they said, 'Don't go up to Jerusalem. Herod is preparing to kill you.' But, 'He stedfastly set his face to go to Jerusalem' (Lk 9:51). Nothing could stop him; he went deliberately. Why?

And there is only one answer to that question. It was all necessary because of sin, because sin had reduced men and women to such a state and condition that nothing could deliver them from it, nothing save the coming of the Son of God into the world and his going to the death of the cross. 'I am not ashamed of the gospel of Christ,' wrote the apostle Paul, 'for it is the power of God unto salvation to every one that believeth; to the Jew first, and also to the Greek' (Rom 1:16).

In other words, you cannot see any point in the Communion service apart from that. There is no point or purpose in believing that Jesus is the Son of God, and that he had to die on that cross, unless we understand the truth about ourselves as men and women in sin. In sin! And it is because this condition, in which we all are by nature and which we manifest so much in our daily lives, is depicted so perfectly in this chapter that I am expounding its message. Why the cross? Because of this.

We have looked at two manifestations of sin. We have seen that it is a terrible power which grips men and women and masters them, turning them into slaves in utter helplessness. Now we must look at verses 18–19 to see the third manifestation.

> Woe unto them that draw iniquity with cords of vanity, and sin as it were with a cart rope: that say, Let him make speed, and hasten his work, that we may see it: and let the counsel of the Holy One of Israel draw nigh and come, that we may know it!

Let us pick out the principles that are taught here.

Notice, first, the deliberate, wilful element in sin. 'Woe unto them that draw iniquity' – they draw it to themselves. This is a very interesting statement, and I am concerned to show its relevance to the present time in which we live. I shall show later on that there is a kind of periodicity in the manifestation of sin. But perhaps nothing is more obvious about it than just this element of wilfulness, this deliberate element: 'They draw iniquity with cords of vanity.'

When he says that, Isaiah means that it was not merely that they fell accidentally into sin. It was not merely that as they were going along in all innocence, sudden temptation came and before they knew where they were they had fallen. No; that does happen, and it is reprehensible, and will be punished, but this is worse. The trouble with the Children of Israel at this particular juncture was not merely that they were falling almost inadvertently into sin because of the weakness of the flesh, the power of sin and the subtlety of temptation – it was worse. They were going out of their way to sin, they were making provision for it, preparing themselves for sin and going out deliberately in order to find it.

This is something which the Bible deals with in many places. The apostle Paul says, 'Make not provision for the flesh' (Rom 13:14). Why? Because the flesh is bad enough as it is. The 'flesh', which means the sinful nature, is so powerful that you need not help it, says Paul. Do not feed it. Do not provide it with any sort of ammunition or any kind of food.

Of course, we all know how true this is. We have a constant fight against 'the world, the flesh and the devil'; it is always there. We were born into such a world. Whatever we may do, sin is there and it is always waiting for opportunities, always ready to attack. And it does attack us; it gets hold of us and gets us down. But these people in the time of Isaiah were actually drawing it to themselves; they wanted it; they went out of their way to meet it and produce it; they were encouraging it for all they were worth. That is the charge that is made against them at this particular point – that they were setting themselves deliberately to sin. They were making provision for the flesh.

Now the word 'draw', which Isaiah uses here, is very interesting. It brings out the element of deliberateness that I am trying to emphasise because it means that they were doing this in spite of certain things. They had to do the drawing; they had to pull, as it were, and therefore exert energy. They had to overcome certain resistances.

What were these resistances? Well, the Children of Israel were having to overcome the resistance of the teaching which they had had as the people of God. These were the people to whom God had given the Ten Commandments through his servant Moses. They were not ignorant; they were not living in the darkness of paganism; they were not unenlightened. They had had incomparable teaching as to how men and women should live: 'Thou shalt not kill; thou shalt not steal; thou shalt not commit adultery' and so on (Ex 20). But in spite of all this ethical teaching, in spite of the fact that God himself had instructed them, they were going against it, and they were going out of their way to do the very things that they had been taught not to do. They were defying the great moral teaching of which they were the heirs.

But Isaiah 5 is also an extraordinary and amazing description of life in the world today. Do we not see this very thing being enacted before our eyes? There used to be a certain standard of morality, but that is being laughed at today; it is dismissed as 'Victorianism' and so on. The great heritage of moral righteousness, the moral teaching which we have inherited as citizens of Britain and other countries, is now being pushed aside and men and women are resisting all that is there in the warp and woof of their very constitution and national life. In spite of that heritage, we are drawing iniquity to ourselves.

But not only were the Children of Israel going against the resistance provided by this unique moral teaching, they were also, at the same time, defying the resistance in the realm of their own conscience. Whether people agree with it or not, there is in every man or woman this inward monitor, there is a conscience. The apostle Paul, again, says that people who had never had the law, as it was given by Moses to the Children of Israel, 'shew the work of the law written in their hearts' (Rom 2:15). And that is why they 'accuse or else excuse one another', and themselves. Everyone has a sense of morality and of moral righteousness, of good and evil, right and wrong, and when we are tempted, then it is the monitor who says, 'Don't! Stop!' Through his servant Isaiah God was convicting the people of Jerusalem of brushing aside their conscience, of deliberately pushing it away, and drawing iniquity unto themselves. In 1 Timothy 4:2 the apostle Paul writes of people whose conscience has been 'seared with a hot iron'. They have resisted it so much that it is more or less dead and no longer speaks.

This is a very important point. We are living in an age, in a generation, when men and women are deliberately sinning, deliberately flouting all that is moral and good and clean and pure and uplifting, deliberately setting themselves out to sin, putting their backs into it, as it were, 'drawing iniquity unto themselves', in spite of all that they have as a moral heritage.

The second element in sin that is brought out here is its deceitfulness, or the worthlessness of the life of sin. Isaiah uses this expression, 'Woe unto them that draw iniquity *with cords of vanity*.' Worthless cords! Here again is a pictorial way of putting a point that the Bible makes almost from beginning to end. Isaiah is exposing and ridiculing the emptiness and the vacuity of the arguments which people always use to try to justify the kind of life which they are living. According to the Bible, sin always uses false and deceitful arguments. Sin is subtle and clever, and it succeeds because people can so easily be fooled.

This is the explanation of the whole story of the human race, is it not? Away back in the third chapter of the book of Genesis we are given an account of the temptation of Eve by Satan, and of how she, in turn, persuaded Adam to disobey God. And the thing that stands out about the temptation, as the apostle Paul reminds the Corinthians, is its subtlety – how the devil with his subtlety 'beguiled'

Eve (2 Cor 11:3). He came along with specious arguments and they were accepted. Sin always draws with cords that really are worthless.

Now, as I said, this is a great point, which is made by the Bible everywhere with regard to sin. The author of the epistle to the Hebrews warns his readers, 'lest any of you be hardened through the deceitfulness of sin' (Heb 3:13). There is nothing in the world more deceiving than sin. That is exactly why the world is as it is. That is why we are all such fools. That is why we will not learn from history. That is why, though we read biographies, they do not help us. We see someone's downfall because of this or that wrong action, and we go and do the same thing. 'The deceitfulness of sin!' 'Cords of vanity!'

Let me summarise it all by putting it in a perfect illustration, in the most vivid picture ever painted of this particular aspect of the matter, namely, our Lord's parable of the prodigal son, a young man who 'drew iniquity unto himself with cords of vanity' (Lk 15). There he was, brought up in his father's home with his brother. He could not have had a better father or a better home; he could not have grown up in better circumstances and conditions. Moreover, his prospects were excellent. He had everything that a man could desire. But, you remember, he left it all, and went away to a far country where he was sure he could live a wonderful life. Eventually he not only became a pauper, but he was actually suffering from starvation, and had to eat the husks with which the swine were fed. Even that was beginning to fail and he was 'down and out'. What could possibly have ever led from one condition to the other? There is only one answer – that prodigal son drew iniquity unto himself with cords of vanity.

What does it mean? Well, observe the false reasoning.

Sin is very clever; it always brings forward its reasons, its arguments. Sin knows us so well; it knows that we like to think of ourselves as highly intelligent people. So it does not just tell us, 'Do this'; it gives us reasons for doing it, and they appear to be so wonderful. But the whole point is that in reality they are specious; they are empty and foolish. The reasoning is always false reasoning. The arguments are always wrong.

Look at it as you have it in Genesis 3 in the case of Eve. 'Hath God said . . .?' asked the tempter. The very tone of voice that he used should have put Eve on guard. When anybody comes to you and says, 'Does God say?' at once you should be suspicious. They should not speak like that of God. But the devil came and said, 'Hath God said' – that you shall not do certain things in the Garden?

Eve gave her reply, and the devil said, 'Of course, you know why he says that? God knows perfectly well that the moment you eat of that tree you will become as gods yourselves, and that is why he tells you not to eat. He does not want you to become as gods; he wants to keep you as underlings, as serfs. He tells you not to eat of that because he knows that the moment you do so, your eyes will be opened, and you will understand as God himself does. You will be equal with him, and no longer subservient. You will rule. You will be gods yourselves. Eat the fruit!'

It was the same argument in the case of the prodigal son. 'This life here at home,' he said, 'is dead. Am I alive at all? This is no life. In that foreign country I have been hearing about, they really do see life – they really *live* there. But here – ugh! Prospects, of course, but it is a life of subjugation to my father and to my brother who is older than I am. I'm not being given my chance. I'm not having liberty. I want life. I want to have room to live. I want my fling!' Thus the prodigal son reasoned with himself at the instigation of the devil.

This is typical of the argument of sin. It comes to us and says, 'If you want to *be* someone, stop reading the Bible, stop going to chapel or church, start doing this or that – this is the way to make your mark. You are no longer a child, you are no longer a baby – prove that you are an adult, show what is in you, assert yourself!' Are not these the arguments? 'Cords of vanity'!

Or it may come to us as 'the thing to do'. What an argument! We must do what everybody else is doing. 'If you want to get on,' says sin again, 'you must do this, you must do that.'

And it comes at another time and says, 'There is no harm in it, why do you say there is? Why shouldn't you do it? This is just a bit of Victorianism, you're behind the times. Be up to date!'

These are the arguments of sin, and they are all specious. This is how people draw sin to themselves, these are the reasons they give. This is to be wonderful; this is to be great; this is to be outstanding; this is the way to get on! Sin never tells us a word about what we are going to lose.

So it is not only false in its arguments and reasoning, it is also false in its promises. It offers us everything, but what does it give us? There it is, back in the Garden of Eden, 'Ye shall be as gods' (Gen 3:5). But were they? In a few moments they were shivering and sheltering behind the trees, terrified and alarmed. Trouble had come down, the chaos had begun, and it has gone on ever since: 'with cords of vanity', promising us the world, but giving us nothing; promising us happiness, but leading to misery.

Oh the misery of a life of sin! Do you not know that already? Read your newspapers and you will see it. The life of sin and of vice is miserable, apart from anything else. It does not give happiness, it is a wretched, sordid life. Instead of giving us the things it promises, it robs us of all that is best in us. It robs us of chastity and purity and honesty and a true and noble conception of humanity. It robs us of our knowledge of God and our relationship to him. Sin offers everything and gives nothing. It takes from us the most precious things, and eventually leaves us with the swine and the husks.

It is not always as bad as that in external appearance, but inside, in the soul, in the realm of the spirit and the mind, it is nothing but that. It strips us of all and leaves us with nothing – empty-handed. All we have lived for, we cannot take with us through death, and there we are, exhausted, finished, with nothing. Sin always works like that; it 'draws iniquity with cords of vanity'.

The next statement is, in a sense, still more striking. 'Woe unto them that draw iniquity with cords of vanity, and sin as it were with a cart rope.' Here is a striking contrast, is it not? I wonder how many people still know what a 'cart rope' is? If you have lived all your life in a city you probably do not, but I am old enough to remember days when carts and wagons were drawn by horses, before the internal combustion engine came into common use. Cart ropes! Big, strong ropes with which you yoked your horse on to a wagon, perhaps a number of horses. There was nothing thicker or tougher than a cart rope. If you wanted something very strong to pull this wagon with its tremendous load – of hay or of anything else that happened to be there – you used a cart rope. According to Isaiah that was the trouble with this nation of Israel, that it sinned, as it were, with a cart rope.

What does he mean? He is referring, of course, to the strength of sin, to the blatant element in sin. He is pointing out that they were sinning with all their might, glorying in it; they were giving themselves to it. It was not, I repeat, a case of people falling inadvertently into sin, caught unawares. No, they went out, their eyes aflame, and they sinned with all their might. They held nothing back – 'with a cart rope'. This is Isaiah's way of describing sin without restraints, sin which is unashamed and open and loud.

There is, of course, an argument at this point. People do not like the hypocrite. All right, I will agree with that. Condemn the hypocrite if you like. But there is something to be said even for the hypocrite – he is certainly better than this sort of person who sins with a cart rope because this is not merely sinning, this is ostentation in sin, this is going beyond, this is sinning in such a way that, as the prophet Jeremiah puts it, 'neither could they blush' (Jer 6:15). There is a complete absence of shame; they are so blatant, they boast of it, they cannot get enough of it and they do it with all their might and main.

Are we not living in an age that is guilty of that? Look how it is organised today. Look at the shamelessness of it all. Look at your television screen and you will see sin unashamed. Nothing is kept back, as it were. They bring it all out and sin with all the energy of their being, and all the intelligence they can command; sinning with a cart rope. And they almost seem to be vying and competing with one another with regard to the depth into which they can descend. There is no decency, no shame, no sorrow for sin and no attempt to conceal it. It is all exposed. The prophet Isaiah is describing the twentieth century quite as much and quite as accurately as he was describing the condition of the Children of Israel.

But come to the last point, the defiance, the arrogance, the blasphemous, the insane element in sin. Listen: 'Woe unto them . . . that say, Let him make speed.' They are talking about God, remember. 'Let him make speed, and hasten his work.' We have already had a reference to this work before. We are told of these people, 'They regard not the work of the Lord, neither consider the operation of his hands' (v. 12). We considered that in verse 2, but here they are going beyond that; they not only do not think of the work of God, they defy it. They stand up and say, 'Let him make speed, and hasten his work, that we may see it: and let the counsel of the Holy One of Israel draw nigh and come, that we may know it!'

Now this is a terrible condition. Do you notice the blasphemy? They take the name of God in vain! In effect, they say to the prophet, 'You are always talking about the Holy One of Israel, well, let him draw near and do what he has got to do – your Holy One of Israel!' They refer to him with sarcasm, with scorn, with bitterness and contempt. That is how they speak about the Lord God Almighty! Not only do they take his name in vain, but they make contemptuous references to his work. The prophet has reminded them of what God has threatened, what he has said he is going to do when men and women live that kind of life, and they say, 'Let him make speed then . . . . You are telling us about the word of God, very well, let him execute his word.' Contemptuous references to the word of God, his moral teaching, his threatenings, his judgements, his revelation of himself, and his holy purpose.

But the most terrible thing of all – and this is where sin reveals itself in sheer madness and lunacy – notice the defiance of the power of God, and the challenge to God to do his worst. 'The Holy One of Israel,' they say, 'and you say that he is the Judge of the world, that he is going to punish the world and judge it in righteousness. Very well, why is he hesitating? Why is he holding back? Why doesn't he do it? Your Holy One of Israel, where is he?'

Let me put all this in its modern form, for this, it seems to me, is the condition of so many people. God and his law and his gospel are being ridiculed. God, to so many, is nothing but a term with which they curse or express some kind of oath. They use the name of God in their common parlance and they do so with contempt. They do not believe his book; they do not believe that he exists at all. They are godless and they banish him out of their thoughts; they treat him and all that is true of him with utter contempt and laughter. He is the joke of the clever people. Whether drunk or sober, it does not matter, they blaspheme his name. You even get it reported now in conversation. There was a time when people did not do that. We knew that certain people could not speak without swearing, without cursing, and without using oaths, we had heard about it, but their words were not reported. But now these adjectives and epithets are used publicly, and the blasphemy and the horror of it all are becoming increasingly evident among us.

But not only that, they defy God altogether. They stand up to him and say, as these people were saying, 'If there is a God, well, let him do something. You preachers say God is going to judge and to punish, but I've been living a life of defiance of him and nothing has happened to me. If he is God, why doesn't he show it? If he has power, why doesn't he reveal it? Let him do his worst.'

That is what the people of Israel were saying. It is the kind of talk that you find reported in the second epistle of Peter. Peter prophesied that at the last times they would rise and say the same thing again. 'Where is the promise of his coming?' (2 Pet 3:4).

'You Christians,' they say, 'you Bible believers, you say that you believe in God and that God is going to judge the world, but where is the promise of his coming? You say he's going to send his Son back into the world to judge the world in righteousness and to destroy evil and to set up his glorious kingdom, but where is he? The centuries are passing and there is no sign of his coming. It's nonsense, rubbish; it's all phantasy and fancy. It's not true. There's no God and nothing is going to happen, so sin and live as you like.'

That is the argument, and that is how mankind has behaved at certain terrible periods in the history of the human race. They have stood up to God and have defied him to do his worst.

'We are not afraid of God! You people are afraid, your religion is a matter of fear, and you are not men. You are nothing but frightened, shrivelled souls. Why not be strong and stand up and say, "There is no God, and God can do nothing"? All the world is in the hands of men and women, and there is nothing to fear. Express yourself, live your own life, have your fling and your fill of pleasure.'

That is the argument, and it is very prominent at the present time. It is being blared at us through the media.

But there are terrible warnings against that sort of thing in the Scriptures. There were certain people when our Lord was here in this world who said a very similar thing: 'When Pilate saw that he could prevail nothing, but that rather a tumult was made . . .' (Mt 27:24) – Pilate had been warned by his wife not to have anything to do with the condemnation of the Lord Jesus Christ. She had said, 'I have had a dream about this man, do not do anything.' And Pilate did his best to set him free. But the Jews would not have that. They said, 'No! Away with this man. Crucify him. Give Barabbas to us.' So:

When Pilate saw that he could prevail nothing, but that

rather a tumult was made, he took water, and washed his hands before the multitude, saying, I am innocent of the blood of this just person: see ye to it. Then answered all the people, and said, His blood be on us, and on our children (Mt 27:24-25).

'We are not afraid,' they said in effect. 'You, Roman Governor Pilate, you seem to be afraid, you are washing your hands of the thing and saying, "See to it yourselves." All right,' they said, 'we are very ready indeed to take the responsibility, we are not afraid. His blood be on us, and on our children. Let him do his worst.'

They said the very thing that Isaiah accused his contemporaries of saying.

That is what they said, somewhere about AD 33. And then came AD 70 when the Roman armies gathered round Jerusalem and sacked it, and murdered and killed these very Jews who had said, 'His blood be on us.' And it did come upon them, their city was razed to the ground and they were thrown out of Palestine among the nations, where the vast majority still are. The blood of Christ has come upon the Jews throughout the running centuries. They asked for it and they got it.

In Isaiah's time the Children of Israel also suffered. Isaiah had warned them, but they did not listen. And so the day came when the Chaldean army surrounded their city and it was destroyed, and they were carried away into the captivity of Babylon. They had said, 'If God can do anything, let him do it.' And he did it.

And my message is that God is still the same. It is all in the third chapter of Peter's second epistle. The scoffers get up and say, 'Where is the promise of his coming? for since the fathers fell asleep, all things continue as they were from the beginning of creation.' Here is the answer:

Beloved, be not ignorant of this one thing, that one day is with the Lord as a thousand years, and a thousand years as one day. The Lord is not slack concerning his promise, as some men count slackness; but is longsuffering to us-ward, not willing that any should perish, but that all should come to repentance. But the day of the Lord will come as a thief in the night; in the which the heavens shall pass away with a great noise, and the elements shall melt with fervent heat, the earth also and the works that are therein shall be burned up (2 Pet 3:8–10).

It is coming! God will act!

But, remember, he does not act immediately; with the Lord a thousand years are as one day, and one day as a thousand years. And upon this present generation, and upon all other generations that have blasphemed the name of God, and ignored and ridiculed his word and his laws, his power shall be manifest, and they shall see his works and feel his power: 'The heavens shall pass away with a great noise . . . .' And all evil and sin shall be consigned to a lake of destruction and of perdition. Oh the blasphemy and the arrogance and the madness of men and women in sin! That is why the world is as it is.

Can anything be done for such people? They draw iniquity unto themselves with all their power, and there they are. Is there any hope? Well, thank God, there is hope. There is only one hope and it is that the power of God is greater even than the power of sin and the devil and hell. Sin and the devil draw us and make us draw iniquity to ourselves with a cart rope, and men and women cannot extricate themselves. But the power of God can.

Listen to God putting it through the prophet Hosea: 'I drew them with the cords of a man, with bands of love: and I was to them as they that take off the yoke on their jaws, and I laid meat unto them' (Hos 11:4). Here is the only hope, the drawing power of God, which is greater than the drawing power of sin. Sin draws with a cart rope, God draws with bands of love and the cords of a man! 'No man can come to me, except the Father which hath sent me draw him' (Jn 6:44). That is indeed our only hope.

What is the hope? It is that God is able to call us out of darkness into his marvellous light! That is the gospel. 'For it is the power of God unto salvation to every one that believeth' (Rom 1:16). He can draw us unto himself. He does it in Christ who said, 'I, if I be lifted up from the earth, will draw all men unto me' (Jn 12:32). This is the blessed good news in this evil world, where sin is drawing us ever more powerfully. But God is yet more powerful: in dying on that cross and giving his body to be broken and his blood to be shed, Christ was liberating a power that is great enough to make the foulest clean. 'Christ crucified . . . the power of God, and the wisdom of God' (1 Cor 1:23–24). It is there. He 'draws'. And if he did not draw us we would all be damned, drawn to hell by sin with cart ropes.

And in the light of that drawing power of the cross of Christ we can say what the prophet Isaiah says in the twelfth chapter: 'Therefore with joy shall ye draw water out of the wells of salvation' (Is 12:3). You who have been drawing sin, draw out of the wells of salvation opened on Calvary's hill. If you have spent your lifetime in drawing iniquity with cords of vanity and with a cart rope, I say now: Give up. 'Draw nigh to God, and he will draw nigh to you' (Jas 4:8).

5

Moral Perversion

Woe unto them that call evil good, and good evil; that put darkness for light, and light for darkness; that put bitter for sweet, and sweet for bitter! (Isaiah 5:20).

It is of the very essence of the understanding of this message – the whole of the chapter, as well as this particular verse 20 – that we should realise that it was a message for the period in which it was uttered. The prophet, let me remind you, was raised up by God to address his contemporaries, the nation of Judah, in particularly serious times. This nation had been in existence for many years, created in Abraham, but now, at this particular point in the eighth century before Christ, things were beginning to go badly, dangerously wrong. The nation was face to face with calamity, and now God had raised a prophet to warn the people that if they did not repent and return to God then nothing faced them but ruin.

But, as we have seen, we are living in an age and in a generation which, alas, corresponds only too exactly to that described here. Furthermore, according to the teaching of the Bible, men and women, ever since they fell and disobeyed God, have always been sinful in all ages and in all generations. But – and this is the principle – there are epochs and times when they are unusually, exceptionally sinful, or when, to put it another way, their sinfulness is particularly evident.

You cannot read the Bible – which is, of course, a book of history as well as a book with great teaching – without noticing that there is an extraordinary kind of periodicity in this respect. You will find ages when the Israelites were certainly not living perfect lives, but they were comparatively good. Then there were other outstanding periods when, as we have seen, they sinned, as it were, with cart ropes, violently, and the whole position became desperate. In other words, at times sin seems to work up to some terrible climax; and that climax is invariably followed by calamity.

In saying that, I am making a simple historical observation. You see this sort of undulating graph in the history of mankind as you read both the Old and the New Testaments, and exactly the same is found as you follow the subsequent history of the human race. Take, for instance, the account which the Bible gives of the destruction of the world in the Flood. This is what it tells us. Adam and Eve's son, Cain, began to sin; his progeny continued in the same way and so sin began to increase. It reached a point at which it became so awful that God addressed the human race and said, 'My Spirit shall not always strive with man' (Gen 6:3). So he raised up a man called Noah to warn mankind that if they did not repent, their world would be destroyed. That generation was one of those generations when mankind sinned with all its might and defied God with unusual arrogance. And it was followed by the calamity of the Flood.

Another instance was in connection with the Tower of Babel. There again, the sin of mankind reached such a height of enormity that God, as it were, came down and confused their language, destroying the Tower that they were trying to erect, and again it led to a disastrous situation. And here, in what we are considering in the book of the prophet Isaiah, we have another notable example of the same thing. Here was Judah sinning in the way that Isaiah describes, heading up to a final orgy, and again it was followed by calamity. The Chaldeans, the Babylonians, arose and, gathering an army together, came and sacked the city of Jerusalem, taking the majority of the Jews away as captives to the land of Babylon. This awful sinning, this terrible period of sinning, again led to calamity.

You get exactly the same thing in the time of our Lord and Saviour. The Jews again began to sin in this exceptional manner. In spite of the warning of John the Baptist, in spite of the warning of the Son of God himself, they would not listen. In spite of the subsequent preaching of the apostles, they continued desperately in sin, and again it led to exactly the same result. In AD 70 the Roman army surrounded the city of Jerusalem, conquered it and sacked it, razing it to the ground, and the Jews as a nation were thrown out among the other nations.

These are illustrations of this principle that is taught so clearly in the Bible, that whereas men and women are always sinful, there are times when sin, as it were, over-reaches itself; it goes mad and people sin in such a desperate manner, defying God in blasphemous arrogance, that it leads up to a period which is almost indescribable in its horror. The Bible teaches us that at such times God withdraws his restraining power and allows human beings to fester in their iniquity, and then he visits them with punishment in the form of some terrible disaster. But he never does that without warning. He always sends his prophets, his messengers, to speak to the people individually and collectively.

At such times nothing is more prominent in the sinful behaviour of the human race than the element dealt with in this verse we are looking at, and that is *moral perversion*. 'Woe unto them that call evil good, and good evil; that put darkness for light, and light for darkness; that put bitter for sweet, and sweet for bitter!' In all these periods in the history of mankind, when sin loses its head, this is invariably the most outstanding characteristic. And it is put before us forcibly here, in this one verse. And it is, alas, because this is the most prominent element in the life of the world at this present time that I am calling your attention to it.

In the light of all this which is demonstrated so clearly by history, is there anything that calls so urgently for our consideration as this? Does anything matter face to face with this? By the side of this, what significance has the greatest conference among world statesmen? If this is true, then we are in a desperate position. If the law of history is true, unless we repent and return to God, there is only one end – calamity. So let us look at the teaching of the Scriptures with respect to this matter.

First, we must consider the characteristics of this condition. The principle is always the same, but I want to put it particularly in its modern expression. Now sin is always sin, but there are degrees of sin. It can appear in different forms and different guises. Sometimes men and women sin and are ashamed of it. That is one condition of sin. But then there are other times, as we have already seen in our previous studies, when people no longer feel shame; they sin openly; they are proud of it and even boast of it. That is different, is it not?

But there is something even beyond that. There are

times when people do not seem to have any moral sense
at all, and this is true not only in general but also of individuals. We have all known individuals who have sinned
and are ashamed of it. I hope that such shame is true of all
of us. We have also known those who have sinned and
have not been ashamed. And we may have known individuals who seem to have lost their moral sense
altogether, who do not seem to know the difference
between right and wrong. They are amoral, non-moral.

But there is something even worse than that – and that
is what is described in this verse, namely, the condition of
perversion. For to be perverted is to be worse than to be
amoral. To be non-moral is at any rate to be negative, but
these have gone beyond amorality to a position in which
they reverse morality and put evil for good, and good for
evil; darkness for light, and light for darkness; bitter for
sweet, and sweet for bitter. This is a condition in which
they have overturned all the standards. It is a deliberate,
positive reversal of what hitherto has been more or less
universally accepted.

This is something that can be seen in individuals, in
nations, in groups of people and sometimes in the life of
the whole world, as I have shown you from the Scriptures. In this state men and women turn everything
upside down and glory in the fact that they are doing so.
That was the condition of the people living in Jerusalem
when Isaiah addressed them in this prophecy and warned
them that unless they repented they could expect nothing
but disaster.

Is not this equally true today? Is not this one of the
most obvious characteristics of these years in which we
are living? Is not this element of perversion the greatest
and the most outstanding characteristic of our times, this
turning upside down, the reversal of everything that has

commonly been accepted and recognised? This can be illustrated in almost every realm; it is a most pervasive condition. You find it in all the arts where beauty is often despised, form and line are not recognised and the ugly is enthroned.

But this perverting of standards is much more serious, of course, when you come to the realm of morals. The great word today, about which people boast, is the 'new morality'. This is being taught quite openly. In December 1962 Professor Carstairs gave his famous Reith Lectures in which he quite blatantly attacked traditional morality and propounded what is called a 'new morality', advocating experiments in sex before marriage, and also extramarital experience. And not only Professor Carstairs, there are also others who do not hesitate to write books and articles and appear on television programmes, introducing this new morality which tells us that what has been regarded as sinful is not sinful. Indeed, they agree that it is wrong to condemn these things, because they are a form of self-expression.

So we are confronted not only by an attack upon religion but also upon morality as a whole, and the attack is blatant and daily. Indeed, it goes further. There are those who even attack the mind of man. That was the essence of the position of D. H. Lawrence. He said that the whole trouble with the human race is that it thinks too much and the cerebrum has developed too much. So the secret of success and happiness in life is to let the lower part govern and take control; 'back to nature', if you like. It is an attack upon the mind and upon everything whereby we exercise discrimination and control. Indeed, to sum it up, it is ultimately a ridiculing of control, of discipline and of decency. It is a plea that we should do anything we want to do, and dismiss any idea of decency and order.

Let me give but one example. I happened to notice a
heading in a newspaper so I read the criticism of a play
that has just started running in London. This is what a
well-known critic said: 'A decade ago on television this
type of wailing among the soapsuds must have seemed
daring and realistic. Its homilies about infidelity and the
sanctity of the family have overtones of middle-class
morality that appear both old-fashioned and prudish.'
That is what we have come to! Apparently this was a play
which ten years ago would have been rather daring and
somewhat shocking, but, by today, any attempt, even fee-
bly, to defend morality or to talk about the wrongfulness
of infidelity, and the sanctity of the family as a unit in
society, is something that is dismissed with great scorn as
'middle-class morality that appears both old-fashioned
and prudish'.

In a sense it is a waste of time to read these criticisms,
in another sense it is not. I read the drama and film critics
and this is what I have observed. If there is any element of
decency in a film or in a play it is dismissed and ridiculed.
That alone is praised which is perverted, which brings in
the abnormal and the ugly, and, more or less, the foul.
That seems to be the universal standard and if there is any
element of romance or of beauty, it is laughed at.

That is the position which confronts us; and you may
have noticed something further. Are you not aware today
of a tendency to be much more sympathetic towards
criminals than towards the people who suffer at their
hands? Pity the poor criminals! People go round petition-
ing on their behalf saying how sorry they are for them
and that they must never be handled too harshly.

And the same applies to perverts. We have almost
reached the stage in which not to be a pervert is to be
abnormal. The pervert is glorified. There is nothing so

wonderful as the love of perverts!

This can all be summed up in the phrase which has become the slogan of the modern generation: 'Evil, be thou my good.' 'Woe unto them that call evil good, and good evil . . . .' That is precisely what is happening in so many countries today in cultured, learned circles, among the intellectuals and those who claim that they are leaders of society. Is it not an exact repetition of the days of Isaiah?

What is the case that the devotees of such perversion attempt to put up for it? I obviously cannot deal with this adequately. I am simply trying to give a bird's-eye view of the whole situation. One of the great lines of justification for all this is that at any rate it is not hypocrisy. Hypocrisy is regarded as the worst thing conceivable; and this is the answer to it – perversion!

Now no one, obviously, wants to defend hypocrisy. There is nothing that can be said, ultimately, in its defence; but that famous utterer of maxims, the French Count de la Rochefoucauld, uttered a truth about hypocrisy. He said, 'Hypocrisy is the homage paid by vice to virtue' – and that is a very profound statement. In other words, a hypocrite is a man who knows he is wrong and is trying to hide that wrong, trying to pretend that he has not done it. He recognises morality and he is, at any rate, paying tribute to it. He is not a pervert. That much can be said for hypocrisy. There is, therefore, always some hope for the hypocrite; he is a twister, but at least he knows that he is wrong.

The second element in the justification of the new morality, or the case put for it, is that it is right to question the existence of any external, objective, universal moral standard. Hitherto, mankind in general has believed that there is such a standard. They have sometimes called it 'natural law', and it has been more or less recognised in all societies, Christian or not. But we are living in an age when that is being seriously questioned and we are being told by some leading philosophers that there is no such thing as an external moral standard, that every man is his own standard. What I think is right is moral for me, and if I do something that you think is wrong, that does not matter, I must act according to my own standard and insight, and there it is. So every man becomes a law unto himself and does what he wants to do, and what he believes it is right for him to do.

Another very serious point is that such people are querying the whole category of the natural, or the normal. The Bible makes a great point of this. For instance, you read in 2 Timothy 3:3, 'without natural affection'. In the same way you have that crucial statement in the first chapter of Romans, where Paul, in his great indictment of the age to which he belonged and of other ages, uses this kind of language: 'Likewise also the men, leaving the *natural* use of the woman, burned in their lust one toward another; men with men working that which is unseemly, and receiving in themselves that recompence of their error which was meet' (v. 27), and so on. The same, he says, is true of women. But the term he uses is 'natural'.

Now today that is being disputed. We are being told that we must not use this term. They ask, 'What do you mean by "natural", and "normal"?' They add, 'What you really mean is, natural for you. But if another man is different, it is not natural for him.' There is no difference, ultimately, between the sexes and there is no such thing as 'natural'. And so this behaviour is being justified by questioning the natural difference between man and woman, and the natural desire of woman for man and man for woman. Indeed, it is all being denied, and it is said that it may be 'natural' for man to desire man, and woman to desire woman. All the standards have gone because the category of the natural is no longer recognised.

And, of course, on top of that, people say that there is no such thing as sin because there is no God. If there are no universal moral canons there is no sin. Indeed, there is no crime. You find increasingly in the courts that a plea is put forward of 'reduced responsibility' or 'diminished responsibility'. What does that mean? A doctor appears in court who says, 'This man has done this – that is admitted – but I am here to say that he could not help doing it because he is made as he is; he is so constituted physically and biologically that he cannot help doing it.' So not only no sin, but no crime; it just becomes a matter of medical treatment. All standards have gone and gone for ever. I grant, of course, that there are scriptural cases where the plea of 'diminished responsibility' is valid, but I am protesting against the tendency to universalise the exceptional.

Then, positively, the justification of wrongdoing takes the form of the cult of self-expression. We are told, 'You have these powers within you, so surely you were meant to use them. These were not meant to be repressed and held back. Why were you ever given them? Why are they in you at all? Exert yourself. Express yourself.'

Then there is the putting up of love against chastity. 'The trouble in the past,' they say, 'has been that chastity has been regarded as the great thing instead of love. But love is what really matters, chastity only comes second. As long as there is love it makes no difference as to whether a man loves a man or a woman sexually. We must not talk about morality and chastity, nothing matters but love.' So you have all the muddle and promiscuity and perversions of today.

Now my problem is to show the wrongness of all that in brief compass. Our Lord puts it like this:

> Thou shalt love the Lord thy God with all thy heart, and with all thy soul, and with all thy mind, and with all thy strength: this is the first commandment. And the second is like, namely this, Thou shalt love thy neighbour as thyself (Mk 12:30–31).

If you look at it like that, you will not justify everything you do simply by saying, 'Oh, I love.' You will recognise that it may be lust, and that you must not harm the other person. You will realise that the other one is a person in the sight of God, that God is over you both and that you are not animals but responsible beings before an Almighty God who meant you to live a higher and nobler life. You will realise that you must therefore discipline and control yourself, and that you express your love by considering your neighbour as yourself, and not by always considering yourself and your desire for self-gratification.

We have considered, then, the arguments that are put forward in favour of the new morality and have seen that they are all specious arguments. They are therefore not the real explanation of modern conduct.

No, the answer is quite simple to those who know their Bible. The first thing the Bible has to say is that there is nothing *new* about the 'new morality'. It is as old as the period before the Flood. It is as old as Sodom and Gomorrah! That is where you get your terms from. And yet twentieth-century people are boasting about their great advances. A new morality? It is as old as sin! The Bible knows all about it, and can tell you more about it than most of these modern books. It is all defined and analysed there. Not only that – and to me this is the most remarkable thing of all – the Bible actually prophesies that this sort of thing will happen, that it will recur from time to time.

Again, to those who know their Bible there is nothing extraordinary about the present position. I am not a bit amazed that twentieth-century men and wcmen with all their sophistication are behaving as they do: the Bible tells me that they will. Have you read our Lord's own prophecy about the last times in Luke 17? 'As it was in the days of Noe, so shall it be also . . . . Likewise also as it was in the days of Lot . . . . Even thus shall it be . . .' (Lk 17:26–30). It is all predicted. Whatever else you may be doing, if you are a follower of the so-called new morality you are not doing anything new, your morality is very old. Indeed, as someone has put it, 'The new morality is nothing but the old morality trying to deck itself up in philosophical terms.'

But the Bible can tell you why it arises and why people behave like this, and that is the important thing. Why are we being afflicted by all this at the present time? Why is this horror facing us day by day? Here are the biblical answers. The main explanation is that sin can never satisfy – never. It pretends it is going to. It says, 'Only once.' But you never stop at 'once'. Sin never satisfies and people therefore become tired of their particular sins and want more. When they have exhausted the whole gamut of known sins they invent different ones and they twist and pervert.

Perversion is always a proof of the failure of sin to satisfy. It is a kind of exhaustion. I once knew a very tragic case of a medical man who had become a drug addict. I remember asking that poor fellow, who had been a student with me, 'How did you ever come to do this?' And he told me that his trouble was that he had always been a heavy drinker, and that he had reached a point where drink did not seem to be able to affect him. But he must have some sensation, so with the failure of drink he started on drugs. And there are thousands of poor drug addicts in this country for that reason alone. Sin always presses people to something further, and when, as it were, the normal ways of sinning do not give satisfaction, they turn to the abnormal. It is just a manifestation of the failure of sin truly to satisfy.

But here is a second reason. Have you ever noticed the contradictory and unintelligent aspect of these perversions? Here are men and women, on the one hand boasting of their great advances, boasting of their knowledge, looking back upon and despising their forefathers of a hundred or two hundred years ago, and still more of a thousand and two thousand years ago. Here is modern society at the height of its knowledge and sophistication and development – how wonderfully it has left all previous generations behind. People, it is said, are too intelligent to be Christians! There they are on the one hand.

But look at them, on the other hand, with D. H. Lawrence denouncing the over-development of one part of the brain, and saying that they think too much and that the way to be happy in this world is to stop thinking and let themselves go.

Not only that, but in spite of all the boasting of its great development, where is modern society going in music and art? It is going back to the jungle, back to the drawings on the walls of the caves. These are facts. But both cannot be true at one and the same time. If the best music is the music of illiterate, uneducated savages, where is sophistication? To be sophisticated nowadays is to go back to the primitive, to the original and elemental. And the same is obvious in every other respect. This is amazing, because it is unintelligent. This is the contradictory element that is always found in sin, that while people are trying to boast that they go forward beyond everybody else, in reality they are going right back to the beginning.

But there is something even deeper about all this. Looked at psychologically, I believe that all this is the result of an uneasy conscience. It is people trying to stifle their conscience, trying to brazen it out. It is fear and unhappiness; it is dis-ease.

Another factor, and to me the most important of all, is that all that we are witnessing is ultimately to be traced to a failure to understand the true nature of men and women, the nature and meaning of life and its end and purpose.

Now I am not merely saying all this in criticism. I am a preacher of the gospel and I am interested in this because I desire people to be saved and delivered out of all this, and to be given true happiness in Christ. I am making this point, therefore, in order to help. I believe that the main cause of this modern perversion is frustration and aimlessness. I do not blame people, in a sense. We are living in this appalling century when we have had two world wars, and nations are still piling up armaments, so young people are tempted to ask, 'What is life? What is living? What am I? Am I just cannon-fodder? Am I just here to be blown up by a bomb? I want to experiment, I want to find out. I may not be here long so I want to get the maximum out of life while I'm here.'

Modern men and women are lost; they do not know themselves; they do not know that they are beings made in the image of God; they do not know how to use their mind and brain, they do not realise that they are unlike the animals. They do not know that they are not meant to be creatures of lust, but are meant to reflect something of the eternal God himself. That is the cause of the trouble –

people do not know that and so they behave in this manner which is such an insult to themselves.

Then on top of all that, this is a lurid demonstration of what the Bible means when it talks about the power of sin – the fact that sin is something which grips and masters people, turning them into slaves. That is why God alone can save us. It is because the devil and hell and sin are so powerful. What an evil thing sin is! Let it work itself out, and you will see where it leads you, not merely to sin and shame, but to sin and no shame, sin and no moral conception at all. Then perversion – light, darkness, darkness, light; bitter, sweet, sweet, bitter; and all the foulness and all the consequences that follow.

At the same time, the state of our world today illustrates that the real trouble with human beings is in the heart. Our Lord said it all: 'This,' he said, 'is the condemnation, that light is come into the world, and men loved darkness rather than light, because their deeds were evil' (Jn 3:19). If you are a follower of the new morality it is not because of your head, it is because of your heart. I have proved that you are not governed by your head. If you were, you would not be contradicting yourself as you do. Your trouble is your heart – you like sin, it is lust, it is an evil heart. That is the real explanation of it all.

Let me ask a question. What is the end to which all this invariably leads? We have already answered that. It leads to the Flood, to the destruction of Sodom and Gomorrah, to the sacking of Jerusalem and the children of God being slaves in Babylon. It leads to AD 70 and the dispersion of the Jews among the nations. It always has and it always will.

Take it in secular history. We have seen that this very thing was the cause of the decline and fall of the great Roman empire. Rome fell because she became rotten in her heart. A canker entered there, and the citizens of Rome became immoral and perverted. Rome went wrong centrally, and the Goths and the Vandals came down and conquered her as a result of that. And this has been the cause of the decline and fall of most other empires since. Authorities writing on this say that ancient societies lost their drive and their power as their morals relaxed. It is always the same. Once people lose their moral understanding of themselves and of life, all their drive, politically, militarily, and in every other respect, goes. They loll in the baths, commit their fornications and adulteries and allow their empires to go to ruin.

I remind you again of the solemn words of the Son of God: 'As it was in the days of Noe, so shall it be . . .' (Lk 17:26ff). Before the final judgement comes, he says, that is how they will be living; they will be marrying and giving in marriage, eating and drinking, buying and selling. They did it before the Flood, they did it before Sodom, they will do so once more before the end. This is what makes our present plight so alarmingly serious. Though modern man does not believe in God, and does not believe in moral standards, though he believes in nothing except himself and his own lusts, it does not affect the situation at all. God is still in his heaven; he is still all-powerful and he is still the 'Judge eternal'. God is still going to bring history to an end and he will end it with judgement and the everlasting destruction of all evil and wrong. The devil and all who belong to him will be cast in to the lake of perdition without end.

'In the last days,' says Paul, 'perilous times shall come. For men shall be lovers of their own selves' – here they are; here it is today – 'covetous, boasters, proud, blasphemers, disobedient to parents' – you see it every day in the newspapers; the New Testament is right up to date –

'unthankful, unholy, without natural affection, truce-breakers, false accusers, incontinent' – they cannot control themselves; they say, 'I can't help it, I'm an animal' – 'incontinent, fierce, despisers of those that are good' (2 Tim 3:1–3) – laughing at morality.

Yes, there it was in the first century AD. They despised this 'middle-class morality' – so prudish, so neat and tidy. They spat upon it; they laughed at it. For men and women to be faithful in marriage, to believe in the family, to restrain themselves – how prudish! How laughable! How behind the times! How outmoded! Fancy still believing in that! Yes, they were 'despisers of those that are good, traitors, heady [swollen up], highminded, lovers of pleasures more than lovers of God' (2 Tim 3:3–4). These are the conditions that always presage calamity and disaster, suffering and woe. And in the name of God I ask you to consider these things in the light of his pronouncement, and in the light of what God has invariably done in the past.

There, then, is the biblical diagnosis. Is there any hope for such people? Is there a message for this world as it is today? Is there anything to say to these 'new moralists', those who gloat and glory in perversion and who ridicule morality and godliness? Thank God, I have a glorious gospel for them. There have been people like this in the world before, as we have seen. The apostle Paul says to the Christians in Galatia, 'Be not deceived; God is not mocked' (Gal 6:7). And to the church at Corinth he says that certain people shall never have an inheritance in the kingdom of God. Who are they? He gives a terrible list, 'Be not deceived: neither fornicators, nor idolaters, nor adulterers, nor effeminate, nor abusers of themselves with mankind . . . nor drunkards, nor revilers . . . shall inherit the kingdom of God' (1 Cor 6:9–10). They are outside.

Nothing unclean can enter into the kingdom of God, for 'God is light, and in him is no darkness at all' (1 Jn 1:5). There is no impurity in heaven. All around God is gloriously pure, it is clean, it is healthy, it is lovely and it is true. And men and women in that unclean condition have no inheritance in the kingdom of God.

The trouble, then, is in people's hearts; can anything be done for them? Well, they cannot do it themselves, for you cannot change your heart. 'Can the Ethiopian change his skin, or the leopard his spots?' (Jer 13:23). He cannot. You cannot give yourself a clean heart; you cannot renew your nature.

But the message of the whole Bible is that God can. Our Lord said to Nicodemus, 'Verily, verily, I say unto thee, Except a man be born again, he cannot see the kingdom of God' (Jn 3:3). What men and women need is a new heart, a new nature, a nature that will love the light and hate the darkness. They need a nature that will enjoy what is sweet and not bitter, a nature that wants to love the good and to hate the evil.

And is not that the problem with all of us? It is our nature that is wrong. We are wrong inside. 'For of the abundance of the heart his mouth speaketh' (Lk 6:45). I am led by my heart and led into sin; the whole trouble is there. By nature I need a new heart, a new outlook, a new desire. How can I get it? Well, I cannot produce it, but I can cry out with David in Psalm 51: 'Create in me a clean heart, O God; and renew a right spirit within me' (v. 10). David said that after he had committed adultery and then murder on top of that. He said he was foul, unclean. 'Thou desirest truth in the inward parts' (v. 6) and it was there he was wrong. Lord, make me something that I am not. 'Purge me with hyssop, and I shall be clean: wash me and I shall be whiter than snow' (v. 7).

Thank God, this is still the same message. I do not despair of modern men and women with their so-called new morality and perversions. The gospel is 'the power of God unto salvation' (Rom 1:16). The apostle Paul preached it in the seaport city of Corinth, down in the dregs, in the vileness, in the riot of evil that was Corinth. He preached it there and it was the power of God in the lives of men and women. 'But ye are washed, but ye are sanctified, but ye are justified in the name of the Lord Jesus, and by the Spirit of our God' (1 Cor 6:11). And thank God, it is still true.

> His blood can make the foulest clean,
> His blood availed for me.
> *Charles Wesley*

6

Humanism

Woe unto them that are wise in their own eyes, and prudent in their own sight! (Isaiah 5:21).

This is the fifth woe pronounced by Isaiah on his contemporaries and it deals with something for which we have a new word today – humanism, the creed of our so-called intellectuals.

The relevance of this verse in general, and in some particular respects, too, to our present condition, is something that should cause us to pause for a moment because it brings out certain truths so very clearly. The first is that it again reminds us that the Bible is a strangely contemporary book. People think it is out of date, and that is why they do not read it. They feel that the Bible has nothing to tell us about life today. But the simple answer is that if you but read the Bible, you will find that it tells you all about the modern world. If you want the best description of life as it is being lived at the present time, go to the Bible, and you will find it. That shows us that this is no ordinary book.

But the Bible also gives us the explanation of *why* things are as they are. It tells us that the essential human trouble is always the same. In other words, as the Bible puts it in the book of Ecclesiastes, 'There is no new thing under the sun' (Eccles 1:9) – nothing at all. There is nothing so futile as the curious boast of modernity that it is 'with it'; of all the boasts that is the emptiest. From the intellectual standpoint there is nothing quite so ridiculous as the way in which people think that modern life is something entirely new. They look back upon people who lived before them, and feel that those people knew nothing about life. They say, 'But we have advanced, we have discovered a new way of thinking and of living!' But all that has happened so many times before and it is all in the Bible.

Modern men and women, with all their cleverness, are incapable of inventing a new sin. The worst forms of vice and evil being committed today are to be found somewhere in the Bible. Nothing new under the sun! This boast and claim of modernity, and the idea that the majority of people are not Christians because they are 'up to date' and 'twentieth-century people', is a most futile and foolish claim. I can understand people who say that they are not Christians and do not accept the message, but they must not say that this is because they live in the twentieth century. There is nothing new about such a rejection of Christianity. People have been rejecting it throughout the centuries, and for exactly the same reasons, as we shall show.

This astounding chapter in Isaiah's prophecy shows us these things very clearly, both the contemporary character of the word of God, and the fact that there is nothing new under the sun. History is most important, and if you study it you will find that it goes round in cycles. We think that we are advancing, but that is an illusion; we are always going round in a cycle. This is seen very clearly in the matter of fashions in clothing, as everybody knows. I was reading in a newspaper the other day of a man who kept a suit a number of years. For a long time he had been ashamed to wear it, but now it had again become the fashionable thing to wear!

This is not only true of clothing – it is equally true in the realm of thought, indeed in every realm. Human beings are never very original; they merely go on repeating themselves and the Bible brings that out in a most extraordinary manner.

What does humanism mean? I cannot give a better definition of it than these words of Isaiah, 'Woe unto them that are wise in their own eyes, and prudent in their own sight!' Humanism is belief in humanity. It is interested solely in men and women without God. It banishes God because it believes that human beings are sufficient in and of themselves. That is the very essence of humanism. Man is the centre of the universe, and there is nothing bigger, and nothing greater.

There are two main types of humanism. There is what is called 'classical humanism', which means that for your guidance in life and your understanding of life, you do not go to the Bible but instead you go back to Greek literature and philosophy, Greek drama and Greek poetry. Classical humanists are people who study these great Greek authors and conduct their lives according to their teaching.

It is no part of Christian teaching to disparage those Greeks; they were truly great men. But classical humanism teaches that there is nothing beyond them and that if you desire wisdom you must go back to the thinking and the meditation of these giant brains of the past. You study them and grapple with them, and try to understand what they thought and what they laid down. Then you try to put that into practice, and that is the way to live a good and harmonious life in this present world.

The other form that humanism takes is what is called 'scientific humanism'. This is the more popular of the two at the present time. The classical represents the poetic, the philosophic and so on, and on the other side there is the scientific outlook, the approach which says that the answer to the problems of the world is not going to come from Greek philosophy or poetry so much as from a scientific understanding of the whole universe, human beings included.

This is the more modern of the two humanisms. It claims that it is new, because the discoveries are at least comparatively recent, going back very little more than some four hundred years at the maximum. By delving into the mysteries of the universe and its constitution you discover the scientific truth about life, and from that you proceed to work out your whole scheme of living.

We must examine this because we are told, here in Isaiah, that this confidence in human wisdom leads to woe. But let us be clear about this. It is no part of the case for the Christian gospel to say anything derogatory of the intellect. Indeed, that is the very opposite of gospel teaching. The gospel places great value upon the intellect. Let nobody think that what Isaiah means is that there is no value in having a brain, or in the ability to use it, or in understanding, or the power of reason and so on. It is not that. There is nothing wrong with the intellect or with wisdom in themselves. Indeed, the Bible tells us that the highest gift that God has given to men and women in the realm of gifts – I am not talking about the soul and spirit but actual gifts – the highest of all the gifts is mind, reason, understanding.

The wonderful thing about human beings is that they can contemplate their own selves; they can analyse them-

selves, evaluate and criticise themselves. This is a tremendous gift, given, according to the Bible, by God. So
we must say nothing derogatory about the intellect,
reason, or the mind. The Christian preacher is not just a
sentimentalist or an obscurantist. He is not just a man
who tells stories and tries to entertain people. He is here
to reason with them, because God has given them minds
which they are meant to use. But, as I am going to show,
the real explanation of the world's trouble is the fact that
people's minds have gone wrong, that they do not know
how to use them properly.

What, then, is the attitude of the Bible to humanism? It
is that while there is everything that is right about the
mind, the reason and the understanding, what is wrong is
that people put their final confidence in the mind. They
are so proud of it that they begin to worship it, they think
that it is sufficient in and of itself and nothing is needed
beyond that. The trouble arises when they begin to boast
of reason and to claim that with their mind they can
encompass the entire cosmos. This statement of Isaiah's
puts it so perfectly – 'Woe unto them that are wise in their
own eyes.' They have put themselves up on a pedestal.
'Look at me,' they say, 'am I not wonderful?' 'Wise in
their own eyes, and prudent in their own sight.' There is
nothing wrong with being wise, but if you are wise in
your own eyes, you are in a very dangerous condition. It
is excellent to be prudent, but if you are prudent in your
own sight, then you come under the condemnation that is
delivered by the prophet.

I trust that that is clear. Far from saying that there is no
value in intellect, I am going to use what little I have and
I am going to ask you to do the same!

Why does God pronounce a woe upon those who are
wise in their own eyes, and worship their brains and

understanding – upon humanists? The first answer is that this is the very essence of their trouble and problem, this is the main cause of all the ills of the human race. Read the Bible and you will find that it says that this was their original trouble, and that it has been their trouble ever since. The temptation that first came to the man and the woman, as we have seen, was: 'Hath God said?' (Gen 3:1). In other words, 'Is God trying to keep you down? Is God trying to stand between you and a knowledge of good and evil? Is God trying to withhold something from you?'

'He is,' said the devil, 'because he knows that if you eat of that fruit you will become as gods yourselves, you will have understanding, you will know everything, you will be equal with God.'

That was man's first sin, and it has been the cause of all his subsequent troubles.

But now let me show it in the New Testament. Take, for instance, what the apostle Paul says in the second half of Romans 1. He puts this very plainly. He is describing why the human race has become what it is, and he says, 'Because that, when they knew God, they glorified him not as God, neither were thankful; but became vain in their imaginations, and their foolish heart was darkened. Professing themselves to be wise, they became fools.' There it is exactly – 'Professing themselves to be wise, they became fools, and changed the glory of the uncorruptible God into an image made like to corruptible man, and to birds, and fourfooted beasts, and creeping things. Wherefore God also gave them up . . .' (Rom 1:21–24). This is a summary of the history of the human race.

In chapter 12 of Romans Paul puts the problem in the form of a piece of advice. We probably all need this advice: 'Be of the same mind one toward another. Mind not high things, but condescend to men of low estate. Be not wise in your own conceits' (Rom 12:16). It is the same thing – the danger of trusting to your own wisdom, your own intellect, the feeling that you are wonderful and need no help at all.

It is found still more clearly in a great passage in 1 Corinthians from chapter 1:17 to the end of the third chapter. Here Paul draws a contrast between the gospel and the wisdom of the wise. Because they were trusting to their own intellects and their own understanding the Greek philosophers were dismissing the gospel as 'foolish'. That has always been the great trouble.

The Bible is full of this teaching. No kind of person was more condemned by our Lord than the Pharisee. The trouble was his conceit. He thought that he was all right, that he was very wise and that he was doing everything perfectly. Pharisees 'trusted in themselves that they were righteous' (Lk 18:9). It is the same thing. They did not need any help and they resented the teaching of this upstart, as they regarded our Lord. Who was he to teach them? Pride of intellect: it was their central trouble, a manifestation of a curious kind of humanism. Christ also taught exactly the same point in his parable of the rich fool in the twelfth chapter of Luke's Gospel.

The case put forward in the Bible is that pride of intellect is, in a sense, the ultimate sin. This is the primary trouble that leads to all the others – men and women glorying in themselves, glorying especially in their intellect and their mind. In 1 Corinthians the apostle Paul explains how this becomes the ultimate sin. It is because men and women misappropriate God's greatest gift. God complimented human beings by making them in his own image, and he gave them this astounding gift. But this is the very thing that they use against God and for themselves, and so bring themselves down.

The second reason why a 'woe' is pronounced on this is that people believe a lie. They think that they are wise and prudent; but they are not. Now this, surely, is a most astonishing fact. Modern men and women are proud of themselves, of their intellect and wisdom; they feel they are superior to all who have ever lived before them. But how can they possibly feel like that about themselves with the world as it is now and as it has been during this twentieth century, with horrible wars, mounting crime waves and utter confusion?

And the Bible explains this by saying that people glory in their wisdom and in their prudence because they are fools! The wiser the man or woman, the more humble they are. It is those who have a smattering of knowledge who are always difficult. Those who really have great knowledge know enough to know what they do not know. 'A little learning is a dangerous thing!' And so the Bible says that the ultimate truth about those who do not believe in God, and who are not Christians, is that they are fools.

The Bible uses many terms in its descriptions of the sinner, but 'fool' is the one it uses most frequently. Our Lord uses it in the parable about 'the rich fool'. Here is a man boasting – 'Soul, thou hast much goods laid up for many years; take thine ease, eat, drink, and be merry' (Lk 12:19–20). The man who thought he was so clever, so wise, was nothing but a fool.

'I'm all right, Jack!' That is the modern way of putting it – 'I'm all right; I've got money put by for the future. I've used my mind. What a clever fellow I am!'

'Thou fool,' says God, 'this night thy soul shall be required of thee: then whose shall those things be, which thou hast provided?' The Bible pronounces 'woe' upon all this because it is a lie.

'But how do you prove that it's a lie?' asks someone.

Unfortunately, I can do so far too easily. I say that those who are wise and prudent in their own sight are to be condemned because they condemn themselves; they are a living lie. They claim to be wise; but how do they live? How do you test wisdom? How do you test intellect and understanding? It is not a matter of reading books and being able to give answers. That is the big mistake people make. No, the way to test people is not by how much they know, but by whether they have the power to *apply* what they know. Do they understand it sufficiently to put it into practice?

I have known many people who were excellent examinees, but who were useless afterwards. I have known people who, as medical students, could do well in examinations, they could learn facts off by heart and recite textbooks like parrots, but, clinically, when face to face with a patient, they were useless; they were quite incapable of applying their knowledge. But that is the test of wisdom.

The wise man or woman does not merely have knowledge – you can put that into computers – they have the power of appropriating and assimilating that knowledge until it becomes judgement. It becomes part of them, controlling their point of view, and determining their actions and practice. So our wisdom is judged not merely by the number of books we have read, or can quote and recite, but by the way we live, the way we use that knowledge. Christ put that in a famous question – 'What shall it profit a man, if he shall gain the whole world [of knowledge and of wealth], and lose his own soul?' (Mk 8:36).

What about human beings individually at the present time? How are the so-called 'wise' men and women living? Look at these people who can tell us all about life. How many times have some of them passed through the divorce courts? Take many of the most famous philosophers. Read their records. Never take people's books alone – find out something about them. To write a book is so easy, very much easier than it is to live! Yes, it is easier to preach than it is to live. But living is the test of wisdom. I am not interested in a man or woman's claim to great knowledge and perspicuity if they are failing in their own lives, if they are drunkards, or adulterers, if you cannot trust them. What then is the value of their knowledge and learning? They say they are wise, but they are not; they are fools, deceiving and deluding themselves.

But what of men and women collectively? How proud the world is of its learning, but look at it! While they are so proud of themselves and their intellect and so on, they must be reminded of these facts. With all their wisdom and knowledge, they have already had two world wars and they have blasted more people to destruction in this one century than ever before. That is what modern men and women with their wisdom and prudence do in practice. And here they are, still arguing about missiles and the means of destruction, still troubled by tensions and insecurity and discord and moral muddle.

Yet people go on boasting about their wisdom. They are wise in their own eyes, and prudent in their own sight – with their world a mess, with a kind of carnage before their very eyes! It is a lie! That is why it is condemned in the Bible. It is just boasting, nothing but talk. It has the bigness of an inflated balloon. It is loud in its profession, but there is no practice.

But I can demonstrate this in another way and that is the failure of people even to understand. They like to think that though they are not perfect saints, as they put it, they do have great understanding. But have they? 'Wise in his own eyes.' So what is your view of yourself?

What is man? Do you understand him? Do you understand yourself? Do modern man and woman really understand themselves? Do they understand the meaning of life? They are so proud of their wisdom and knowledge, but what do they really tell us about life? Is it big, or is it little? Is it something grand or something ignoble? What is it?

Where, then, is their understanding? Where do they show their prudence and their wisdom? What is the whole meaning of the world? What is history? Is there any design in it at all or any purpose? Or is it all just a bag of nonsense, pointless, purposeless, just blundering along in any direction without anyone knowing where or what or how? Where is the wisdom in all this? What do men and women know about the most important things? They know a great deal about electricity and the atom and power, and all these abstruse scientific matters. I do not criticise that, but when you are talking about wisdom, what I want to know is: How do I live? What is it all about? How can I find happiness and peace? How can I live in such a way that I shall not be ashamed of myself at the end of my journey? That is wisdom, that is prudence.

But, further, people do not seem to know anything about the cause of their problems. These people who have been 'wise in their own eyes, and prudent in their own sight' for the last hundred years have been prophesying wonderful things for us in this century. We were going to solve all our problems. The Victorian thinkers – the philosophers, the poets, the politicians, the agnostics – all said this. The trouble with men and women, they said, was that they were too poor, and crime was inevitable while you had poverty. But once people were educated, once you gave them good houses and better salaries, everything would be put right. Well, we have dealt with most of those defects yet the problem is greater than ever – indeed, we are now told that the rising crime wave is due to affluence! Where is the wisdom? Where is the prudence? People obviously do not understand their problem, still less are they able to discover a cure.

I am told that I must not criticise modern dramatists and novelists. I am told that they are moralists who are trying to improve conditions. But what is their method? Their method of trying to improve is to describe. But surely you do not solve a problem by simply describing it; you do not improve a situation simply by painting it? The business of the moralist is to solve the problem, to get us out of the predicament. We do not need any more descriptions. We know all about it. There is no need for anybody to write a book to tell us how people sin: it is all to be found in the Bible. And not only is it all there, but anybody who has lived in this world knows something about it. We do not need novels and films and dramas to tell us how people behave. What we want to know is how to get out of moral failure and confusion, how to stop doing wrong, how to be delivered.

But I am told that the work of modern writers and dramatists is very realistic! All right, but that makes no difference. What would you think of a doctor who, the next time you are taken desperately ill, comes to you and gives you an account of your temperature and your pulse rate and your respiration rate and the colour of your skin and the state of your pupils and so on, who describes your condition to you in a vivid manner and says, 'That is your condition, very serious, very bad' – and then goes home?

That is not a caricature of modern pundits, that is exactly what our humanists are telling us today. I will grant them this, they are experts at description. They can tell us all about ourselves, and analyse the condition for us. 'There you are,' they say, 'that is your condition.'

But they have nothing to give us. Why? Because nothing is higher in creation than human beings, and it is they who have failed.

Take yet another reason why the Bible pronounces a woe upon the humanist. This is much more serious. It does so not only because humanism is a lie, but because of what it produces, because of what it leads to. This is the really serious aspect of the matter. So what is it? First and foremost, it is pride itself. Pride is the greatest of all sins. It is more prolific in causing trouble than anything else in the world. It is also the ugliest of the sins, and what havoc it has caused in the long history of the human race.

And what we are examining is nothing but pride of intellect. It shows itself in the despising of all who have gone before, and modern scientific humanists are very fond of doing that. Nobody knew anything until *they* arrived on the scene. They despise their forefathers. This is seen in every realm. They dismiss all previous books, all previous knowledge. Everything is out of date; nothing is of any value. Indeed, there are foolish people who occupy Christian pulpits who are really saying that, in effect, nobody could truly understand the Bible until this generation with its modern knowledge. They dismiss nineteen centuries of Christian exposition and Christian learning. That in itself is enough to put them out of court – their colossal conceit and pride. It is ugly. And God hates it. He sees man standing up and inflating himself, and he pronounces his woe upon it.

Then that in turn leads to self-confidence and self-satisfaction. Our Lord has painted the perfect picture of this in his parable of the Pharisee and the publican who went up into the Temple to pray. Look at that Pharisee walking up right to the front. Here is a man who is pleased with himself, a man who has a mind and a brain; and he thanks God that he is what he is. He does not need any help; he does not ask for anything. He has everything; he can do everything himself! That is the kind of man whom Christ denounced most bitterly. 'Woe unto you, scribes and Pharisees, hypocrites!' There is nothing more terrible in the sight of God than self-confidence.

But what makes this self-confidence such a terrible thing is that it always leads to rebellion against God. I reminded you earlier on that that was the cause of the original sin. The devil came and said, 'God is trying to hold you down.' And Adam and Eve believed him and began to feel a hatred of God. They felt that if only they could get that knowledge, then all would be well, and they would be able to lead an independent life. So they elevated themselves in their own esteem, and human beings have been on that pedestal ever since.

Rebellion against God – that is the essence of humanism. The humanist says, 'I do not believe in God and I will tell you why. I do not need him. I can carry on perfectly well without him. There is no God.'

God's comment on that is found in Psalm 14: 'The fool hath said in his heart, There is no God' (v. 1). But there are many people today who think that nobody ever said that until this century. But David said that in Psalm 14 nearly three thousand years ago! It was true at that time, a thousand years before Christ was born. People were saying, 'There is no God,' and David said, 'Yes, they say that because they are fools.'

So humanists do not believe in God because, they say, we have no need of him. Why do people who are wise in their own eyes, and prudent in their own sight, need God? If they understand everything and can manage themselves and all life, well, they do not need God. That has increasingly been the position of the human race for the last hundred years, with knowledge growing and advancing and the various developments in scientific knowledge – we are all so advanced!

'Of course,' they say, 'there may have been a time when people needed God, but not now.' Everybody has enough now. We have the money, we are getting better wages, we can get all we want! We can read, we have television sets, and we are men and women of knowledge. So we do not need God.

That is rebellion against God. 'The carnal mind is enmity against God: for it is not subject to the law of God, neither indeed can be' (Rom 8:7). That is always an immediate consequence of rebellion against God. The moment people think they are wise, and rebel against God, they begin to go wrong morally. This is a very subtle matter. Men and women in their folly do not realise that their real objection to God is that they have to obey him, that God is a God of justice, of righteousness and holiness. And the Bible tells us that God made man and woman in his own image, and he meant them to live in the same sort of manner as God himself.

But people do not want to live like that; they do not want to live upright, pure, disciplined and holy lives. They want to give rein to their passions and lusts. Desire, that is the trouble; forbidden fruit, of course. The illicit – ah! This is love!

'Of course, stupid people don't understand,' they say. 'I thought I was in love before, but this is the real thing. I have it now. I thought I had, but I hadn't – this is true love!' Let them do what they like; let them commit adultery and spit upon the sanctities. 'Don't talk about law,' they say, 'don't bring in morality. That's legalism. Love!'

The truth is, of course, that it is nothing but lust, but to suit their own lust and deaden their own conscience, they try to work out a philosophy, and in that philosophy there is nothing higher than human beings. There is no God, so they have nothing to fear; all is well and they can go on pleasing themselves.

There has never been any form of humanism without moral declension. The humanists I know claim to be moral – and in their own personal lives many of them are moral people – but the teaching of the Bible is that in every period when humanism has been in the ascendant, morality has invariably gone down. 'Professing themselves to be wise, they became fools,' says Paul, as we have seen, in Romans 1:22. Then the moral declension came in.

> Wherefore God also gave them up to uncleanness through the lusts of their own hearts, to dishonour their own bodies between themselves: who changed the truth of God into a lie, and worshipped and served the creature rather [in AV margin] than the Creator, who is blessed for ever. Amen. For this cause God gave them up unto vile affections: for even their women did change the natural use into that which is against nature (Rom 1:24–26).

It is a recognised fact of history that some of the great Greek philosophers were moral perverts. High idealists, writing their blueprints of a Utopia, and yet guilty of the foulest vices! It always happens! The moral consequences always follow, and that is why God pronounces woe upon it. When people set themselves up as the final authority they always descend into the abyss. Why? Because they cannot extricate themselves, they have not got the power.

This leads us to the last point, which is that God pronounces 'woe' upon this pride of intellect, this confidence in human understanding, because it is that which above everything else causes men and women to refuse God's way of salvation. This is the most calamitous thing of all. There they are in their awful plight and they try to extricate themselves. They perfect their educational systems, they multiply their cultural media. Never have they been so busy trying to put themselves right as they have been during the last hundred years. They have exhausted almost every conceivable approach and tried every avenue, but in spite of it all we see what is happening. And yet, in this very situation, when the gospel of Christ is offered to men and women, this gospel which alone can deliver them and set them free and save them, they refuse it.

Why is this? It is because they feel that they are sufficient, because they think that they are wise and prudent, because they still think that they can save themselves. Why do people not read history? Why do they not read their own books? History proves that men and women cannot deliver themselves, try as they will, with all their might and main. All great civilisations have gone down, and the present civilisation is going down. But people still refuse the offer of the gospel. They still laugh at Christ and ridicule the cross. They spit into the face of God and say they do not need him. This pride of intellect, this is the curse, this is the real trouble with humanity. They say, 'I will not believe unless I can understand.' They want to understand God! They think they are so big that they can measure God himself, they can measure Infinity!

So men and women are under the wrath and the woe of God, finally, because they refuse God's offer.

God so loved the world, that he gave his only begotten Son,

that whosoever believeth in him should not perish, but have everlasting life. For God sent not his Son into the world to condemn the world; but that the world through him might be saved. He that believeth on him is not condemned: but he that believeth not is condemned already, because he hath not believed in the name of the only begotten Son of God. And this is the condemnation, that light is come into the world, and men loved darkness rather than light, because their deeds were evil (Jn 3:16–19).

God pronounces a woe on all that; and I see calamity coming. More than ever before, men and women are standing up in their pride: proud of their own wisdom, wise in their own eyes, and prudent in their own sight, saying they do not need God and that they can handle and order their own affairs. They maintain that they can perfect the world and they stand up and say all this, while refusing the gospel, ridiculing it and blaspheming against it! They are like that rich fool who turned to himself and congratulated himself, saying, 'Soul, thou hast much goods laid up for many years; take thine ease, eat, drink, and be merry' (Lk 12:19).

'It's a good world,' they say, congratulating themselves. 'We're having a great time. Never had it so good!'

'But God said unto him, Thou fool, this night thy soul shall be required of thee' (Lk 12:20).

What if some scientists are right, and this universe has not got many more years to go, what then? Where is your wisdom and your learning – where is it all? When God says, 'Now, this night you must go out of this world, you must die' – whether of a virus infection or by bomb does not matter, but you have got to die – 'This night thy soul shall be required of thee.' What then? Do you know where you are going? Do you know what happens to you after death? Can you tell me what happens in that 'great unknown' beyond? Here is wisdom – what am I? How do I live? How do I die? What happens to me afterwards? Where is your knowledge? What are you boasting of? The humanist has nothing, nothing at all, and God pronounces his 'woes' upon it, and he does so in a very terrifying manner.

Let me direct your attention to some verses in the book of Revelation, which is the last book of the Bible, the book which tells us of the day that is coming when God will arise and say, 'This night!' to the whole universe. And the great men of the earth, we are told:

> . . . cried when they saw the smoke of her burning [this great city of Babylon, meaning civilisation], saying, What city is like unto this great city! And they cast dust on their heads, and cried, weeping and wailing, saying, Alas, alas, that great city, wherein were made rich all that had ships in the sea by reason of her costliness! for in one hour is she made desolate. Rejoice over her, thou heaven, and ye holy apostles and prophets; for God hath avenged you on her. And a mighty angel took up a stone like a great millstone, and cast it into the sea, saying, Thus with violence shall that great city Babylon be thrown down, and shall be found no more at all (Rev 18:18–21).

And this Babylon of civilisation is going to be destroyed in an hour when God arises. 'Woe unto them that are wise in their own eyes, and prudent in their own sight!'

Is that the last word? Thank God, it is not. But that is the last word as far as humanism is concerned. It is wrong, essentially. It is a fraud. It is deceit. It is a failure. It can do nothing. And it calls down wrath upon itself. But it is not the last word. In spite of this insanity of men and women, in spite of the fact that they are such blind

fools, God has mercy upon them. There is an answer to it
all.

'The fear of the LORD is the beginning of wisdom' (Prov
9:10). That is the answer. People must be awakened; they
must realise it. They must see that they are fools, that they
are failures and that their outlook and life will lead to a
fatal end. And they must submit. The apostle Paul says,
'If any man among you seemeth to be wise in this world,
let him become a fool, that he may be wise' (1 Cor 3:18).
Human wisdom leads to nothing, but there is this 'wisdom from God'.

'We preach Christ crucified, unto the Jews a
stumblingblock, and unto the Greeks foolishness; but
unto them which are called, both Jews and Greeks, Christ
the power of God, and the wisdom of God' (1 Cor 1:23–
24).

'For after that in the wisdom of God the world by wisdom knew not God, it pleased God by the foolishness of
preaching to save them that believe' (1 Cor 1:21).

When men and women had completely failed, 'God
sent forth his Son, made of a woman, made under the law,
to redeem them that were under the law' (Gal 4:4–5).

So what is necessary? Those who want to be wise must
become as little children and admit that they know nothing. Let each one say, 'I am but a child. I thought I knew
but I was just fooling myself. I was drunk on my own
intellect. When it comes to the point, I see that I know
nothing about myself. I don't understand life, I don't
understand the world and I cannot do anything about it.
I cannot control myself and I see everything going wrong.
I'm a fool, a child, I know nothing!' Blessed are those
who come to that position. 'Except ye be converted, and
become as little children, ye shall not enter into the
kingdom of heaven' (Mt 18:3).

And to such people, God says, 'I sent my only begotten Son into the world to redeem people like you. You have become as a little child, so I offer you in Christ my Son, who bore your sins in his own body on the tree – I offer you free forgiveness. I will blot out all your sins as if you had never committed a sin in your life.' God's wisdom in Christ! That is the way to solve the problem. This is heavenly, this is divine wisdom.

7

Sin in High Places

Woe unto them that are mighty to drink wine, and men of strength to mingle strong drink: which justify the wicked for reward, and take away the righteousness of the righteous from him! (Isaiah 5:22–23).

We are looking here at the sixth and the last of the 'woes' that were pronounced by the prophet Isaiah upon his contemporaries. The prophet, let me remind you, was delivering one of his great messages to the nation. It was not his own meditation upon the situation that made him speak. No prophet ever spoke as the result of his own cogitation. 'No prophecy of the scripture,' says Peter, 'is of any private interpretation' (2 Pet 1:20).

That does not mean that we cannot interpret it privately. It means that it did not come into being privately, it is not a man's 'private interpretation'. It is not a great philosopher speaking. It is not the seer looking at the position, meditating upon it, coming to conclusions and then speaking. That is not prophecy. Prophecy is a message given by God to one of his servants, and the whole purpose of God in raising up prophets was that the people might be saved from disaster and the consequences of their own folly. So

we have been looking at this great message, not because
we are animated by any merely historical or antiquarian
interest – although if you really want to do something
intelligent and interesting, there is nothing better than to
consider the story of the Children of Israel; it is much
more exciting than anything fictional.

But we are not considering this passage for that reason;
we cannot afford such luxuries because we are in too
much trouble ourselves. Our business is to listen to this
message of God through his prophet because this message
is always contemporary and as we have been going
through it, we have seen more and more clearly that we
are listening to a word that is also addressed to us at this
present hour. So we come here to the last of the 'woes'
pronounced by the prophet in these extraordinary verses.

Now some of you may think that this is a repetition of
what Isaiah said previously in the second woe: 'Woe unto
them that rise up early in the morning, that they may follow strong drink; that continue until night, till wine
inflame them!' Or you may think that it has something to
do with the fourth of these woes: 'Woe unto them that
call evil good, and good evil; that put darkness for light,
and light for darkness; that put bitter for sweet, and sweet
for bitter!' On the surface it may sound as if this sixth
woe is just a repetition and a kind of confirmation of
these.

But I want to show that that is not so. There is an
element, of course, which is the same, but it goes much
further. It carries the analysis of the condition of the Children of Israel right to its utmost point, for what we have
in these two verses is the manifestation of the sin of Judah
in her greatest leaders, in her judges. They are guilty,
Isaiah says, not only of giving way to drink, but also of
injustice and a loss of moral sense. That is the position

here, licentiousness and injustice in the highest quarters. The 'woe' is pronounced upon men who are guilty of these two things, and I am concerned to show that they go together.

As we look at these 'woes' – and we must summarise them now as we are looking at this last one – we must have been struck and impressed by the protean character of sin. Sin is a terrible disease and its symptoms are almost endless in number. This message stands out in the Bible. The Bible shows what human beings in a condition of sin are capable of, and the variety of the manifestations of sin – we have had a collection of them in this one statement. But they are all due to the same thing and arise from the same source. There is nothing more extraordinary about sin than just that, and it is because of this varied character of its manifestations that people so often do not recognise them as sin at all. The tendency of all of us by nature is to regard certain things only as sin, and we are not aware that other things, which seem to be so different, are equally sinful.

Take, for instance, the way this is put in the Gospels. Two classes of people were having dealings with our Lord – publicans and sinners, and Pharisees and scribes. You feel at first that they have nothing in common. And yet the main thrust of our Lord's teaching was to show that both classes were equally sinful. That is what so infuriated the Pharisees. They recognised that the publicans, that is, the tax-collectors, and the harlots were sinners. Of course! Everybody knew that! But the Pharisees never imagined that they themselves were sinners, that they were suffering from essentially the same disease. Why not? Because they did not manifest the same symptoms; they were not guilty of the same actions. But this selfsame disease can produce a great variety of different manifestations.

In other words, self-righteousness is as much a manifestation of sin as is profligacy and riotous living. Both are
manifestations of the same essential condition, because
sin, ultimately, is a wrong relationship to God and it does
not matter what form it takes. As long as it is a wrong
relationship to God, it is sin. It may be highly respectable,
it may be shameful and obviously disgraceful – it does not
make the slightest difference. Indeed, I could put up a
very good case for arguing that in the sight of God
respectable sin is much more terrible than the other. But
the point I am making is that we are shown here how sin
can be so subtle and variegated in its manifestations that it
eludes us and deludes us, and makes us think that we are
not sinners at all. So the prophet, in the wisdom given to
him by God, does not just say, 'You are sinners,' but he
says, 'You are sinning in this respect and that and that and
that.' He shows the wide character of sin, he brings it
home in detail to individuals, and yet he shows that it is
common to all. That has emerged from our study of this
passage.

Another thing that has come out clearly is the terrible
power of sin. I propose to deal with that in particular now
because it seems to me that this is what our own generation completely fails to understand. This is desperately
serious because the power of sin is the main cause of most
of our present troubles. This comes out particularly strik-
ingly in this last of the 'woes'.

Now modern men and women do not like the term
'sin' at all. The whole notion of sin has been hated in this
present century. I am often amused to observe how some
men who have spent most of their lives in pulpits
denouncing the biblical teaching concerning sin are now
getting rather excited about the social manifestations and
consequences of the sin whose existence they have denied

for so long. If it were not so desperately serious and tragic, it would indeed be really funny. These people have never understood the power of sin. They have told us that we must not say that sin is a positive force and power; what we should say is that certain qualities are lacking. We must not say that a man is a bad man, but that he is not a good man.

Sin, we are told, is a negation; it is the absence of qualities. The pundits with their psychological knowledge teach us that men and women have been misled throughout the centuries by this biblical teaching concerning sin. The truth, they say, is simply that humanity has not developed yet. The human race is like a child who does not realise what he will come to know later, but he will grow up and will then stop doing certain things. What has been called bad or evil is a characteristic of the infancy of the human race, and therefore it is something with which we have to be patient. We must not denounce it or pronounce 'woes' upon it as Isaiah did. That is terrible! That was 'the god of the Old Testament' whom they hate so much because he pronounced woes and judgement.

No, you have just got to be patient with people, they say, and you must show them the beautiful. So you give them portrayals of the beautiful and you tell them moving stories. You do so, perhaps, with a sentimental, affected voice, and you manipulate coloured lights so as to try to produce a psychological effect and make people feel nice and comfortable and happy. In that way they will soon be living better lives.

But now the very teachers of this false doctrine are themselves beginning to get alarmed as they see the increasing evidence of the breakdown of morals. What they fail to realise is that the most powerful force in the world, next to the power of God, is the power of the devil, the power of sin. People talk about atomic power, it is nothing compared with sin. I know that the explosion of an atomic bomb can bring much chaos and calamity, but consider what sin has done to the human race! Here is the great power in human life that has brought wretchedness so constantly, and now threatens to engulf us in a final disaster.

No, sin is not negative; it is not merely the absence of certain qualities. So it cannot be dealt with easily by education and exhortation. The problem of sin cannot be solved by the setting up of more royal commissions. But that is what the authorities are still proposing. Take, for instance, a recent British Medical Association report. Here was a committee that had been sitting for two years and had then brought out its report. The report stressed what medical officers of health have been reporting for some time, that venereal diseases are increasing with terrible rapidity in all countries. What can they do about it?

Ah, they want to call a conference! The educational authorities and the sociologists must come together with the Church – all who teach morality. (That is, incidentally, their idea of the Church – a place where morality is taught.) They must all come together in conference and try to devise some scheme whereby this can be dealt with.

Now all this fatuity is solely due to the fact that they have never realised that sin is the greatest power in the universe apart from the power of God. We live in a world in which these two great powers are fighting a battle for the souls of men and women, for you and for me. We are not faced with some academic problem. These matters are not of mere theoretical interest. We are all vitally, indeed tragically, involved in this. There are parents who are involved because their children are in grievous trouble. The children themselves find their young lives are being ruined. Terrible things are happening and worse things can happen. We are all involved. So the essence of wisdom is to listen to the biblical message in order that we may learn something of the awful, terrible power of sin.

The last of Isaiah's 'woes' reveals the power of sin in a particularly striking manner. The first thing we learn here is that sin is no respecter of persons. That has been another great fallacy. People used to think that you only had sin in certain places. But sin is as common in an affluent suburb as it is in a slum. The truth about sin is that it is common everywhere. In this 'woe' we are told that it affects the highest in the land, the judges, the men to whom you should look for righteousness and for equity and for a just opinion. 'Woe unto them that are mighty to drink wine, and men of strength to mingle strong drink: which justify the wicked for reward, and take away the righteousness of the righteous from him!'

Isaiah puts it like that, of course, in terms of his own civilisation. But we shall look at this in its contemporary form. Sin is no respecter of persons, so if you think that you can divide men and women into those who are sinners and those who are not, and that those who are not sinners are like that because they belong to a certain class, or because of their birth or their ability or their education, you are guilty of a very great fallacy. For the message, here and everywhere, is that no one has a natural immunity to sin. It is so powerful that it can attack the greatest and the mightiest and bring them down in defeat and shame.

The Bible constantly repeats that message. Of course, most of these modern authorities do not like the Old Testament because they say that it is not quite a decent book. We read there about David committing adultery and murder, and you cannot teach things like that to children! But why does the Bible tell us about the adultery of David? It is to show us the power of sin. Here is the king of Israel, a great man at that, and a mighty warrior, a great psalmist and a wonderful poet, but sin got him down. Thank God for an honest book! Here is your BMA report – and all other reports – antedated by many centuries. There is nothing new in all this. When are we going to wake up? When are we going to start reading the Bible, if merely for its history, and cease thinking of ourselves as if we were some special people because we live in the post-war world and in the atomic age? When are we going to grow up and face the facts of history? Here is the great record: that sin attacks everybody, that nobody is immune.

'Do you mean by that,' asks someone, 'that people's ability and education do not count, that birth and up-bringing make no difference?' My reply is that all they do is modify the manifestations a little. The essential trouble remains, the disease is still there. We are good at medicating symptoms, but we are very poor at treating the disease. Nobody is immune to sin. High and low, rich and poor, learned and ignorant – all are its victims. Learning, know-ledge, education are nothing but a cloak. The heart of man remains what it was –

> The rank is but the guinea's stamp;
> The man's the gowd for a' that!
> A man's a man for a' that.
>
> *Robert Burns*

Poor Robert Burns; he knew it. He knew it in himself, and he knew that it was true of others. 'The rank is but the guinea's stamp.' You vary the dress. You sin in even-ing dress rather than in rags, and you think it is different. Thus we fool ourselves; thus humanity and civilisation go on fooling themselves. The 'heart', the inner self, is what matters, and that is the same in all types. Isaiah states that the judges of Israel have gone wrong – the learned men, the men of whom you could expect something better. But sin is no respecter of persons.

I shall never forget the shock I received many years ago when as a young professional man I had the privilege of attending a dinner party of learned men in a certain profession. To my amazement, I found these able men, men in prominent positions, spending a part of their time repeating so-called 'jokes'. I did not expect it in such circles. I foolishly had not understood this message of Isaiah. I thought that it was only a certain class of person who did that sort of thing. I thought that you found that only in the bar parlours of life, that it was confined to the illiterate and the uneducated. But here I was suddenly listening to men in these learned circles spending their time repeating things which the fifth chapter of the epistle to the Ephesians tells us 'should not be named among you'.

I also remember another occasion years later – I am mentioning these things solely in order to illustrate this point – when I found myself in Claridges Hotel, again at a dinner. I had been invited because I had once worked closely with the honoured guest of the evening. It was a gathering of some thirty men only, who had been carefully selected. We first had dinner and then came the speeches. Again I was shocked. The man sitting on my right – a highly qualified expert professional man – was literally sick upon the floor during the dinner, apparently due to the fact that he had consumed too many cocktails on an empty stomach.

You can look at life today in the highest circles, professional, industrial, political and so on, you can go to the most prestigious universities, many of which were originally founded as Christian institutions, and you will find sin rampant, not only among the undergraduates but among their teachers also. Nothing that civilisation has ever produced has succeeded in dealing with the problem of sin. I say that deliberately because civilisation has been humanity's attempt to overcome that problem. Humanity does not put it like that, of course, because it does not believe in sin, but that is what it has been attempting to do. Civilisation has tried to produce order out of the chaos, it has tried to lessen and to mitigate certain wrongs, injustices and suffering, but everything that civilisation has tried to do up to date has completely failed to deal with this terrible power. Nothing is more urgent, more vital, than that we should realise that sin is as powerful as that, and we must rid ourselves once and for ever of the notion that anything that human beings can do can deal radically with it. It cannot. That, as I have shown, was the essential sin of Pharisaism.

Secondly, the terrible thing about the power of sin is also shown in this way: it makes men and women insult their own nature, their own self, their own true greatness and glory. Where does Isaiah say that? It comes out in a very striking way in these two verses. Look, for instance, at what people boast of. Verse 22 is a very remarkable statement. Another translation of it is: 'Woe unto them who are heroes at drink, and strong in mixing wine!' This is a tremendous indictment of those who are guilty of sin. What do they regard as real strength, something of which they can boast? As it was in the time of the prophet Isaiah, so it is today. Men and women have faculties and powers, they have brains and ability, they have physical strength, but what are they proud of? Well, one of the things is their knowledge of drink.

This is not romancing. One of the most popular men appearing on television never fails to boast about his drinking. He does not believe in God; he ridicules Christianity. What does he boast of – this sophisticated man of the world? What, to him, is good living? He has told us repeatedly. It is good food, and then, with a smile, good drink, and good conversation. That is the good life, the real life! That is the cultivated, the civilised life. People boast of that; it has become 'the thing to do'. Your knowledge of drink is the hallmark of your status as a civilised being. If you do not know what wine to have with each particular course in your meal, you are a fool, an ignoramus, you have not 'arrived', you are not 'with it'. Fancy not knowing what to have with the fish course or with the meat! Who are you? Where do you live? Where were you educated? This is the way in which you estimate and judge a person today.

But there is the other element – I want to show how up to date Isaiah is – 'Men of strength to mingle strong drink!' Now I am not talking, let me repeat, of the man in the street, but of those to whom we should look up as leaders. What do they boast of? They boast of the fact that they know how to mix a cocktail! 'Mixing strong drink.' 'Mixing' – the very same term. Not everybody knows how to do it so this is the thing to boast of, this is the hallmark of sophistication.

What else? Ah yes, they are 'men of strength to mingle strong drink, they are mighty to drink wine'. How do you estimate the strength, not of an animal, but of a man? The modern way is to ask, 'Can he carry his liquor?'

Again, I am not romancing; these are sheer facts. I have heard distinguished men boasting of the amount they could drink, that they were the last to remain on their seats when the others had fallen to the floor. There are things that should make us laugh, but not that. Never laugh at drunkenness or at a drunken man. Much havoc and misery in this world is wrought by that. But they boast of this, and they were doing the same in the days of Isaiah. 'Woe' is pronounced on that kind of thing.

What else? Notice that sin in this way makes people insult their own nature in that they obviously fail to find pleasure without indulging in these artificial stimulants and aids. Why do people do that sort of thing? It is because they are miserable without it. They have failed to find happiness; they have failed to find peace; they have failed to find even pleasure. This is to me the most astonishing aspect of sin, and the most insulting to human nature. We are being told that you cannot be convivial without drink, that you have to be 'loosened up'. Are men and women such that they cannot be convivial or pleasant, cannot be happy except under the influence of drugs? But that is the position today. It shows the utter bankruptcy and emptiness of life without God and without Christ. They cannot live without stimulants. So you have your cocktails, your pep pills, your drugs. People do it, they say, to get a kick. Why? Because they are so miserable, so unhappy, and so completely bankrupt emotionally and spiritually.

In the name of human nature, I protest! Men and women do not have to sink so low that they cannot find pleasure unless they drug themselves and bombard their brains and insult themselves. But it all results, as we have seen previously, in knocking out the highest centres of the brain and allowing that which is elemental to take charge.

But notice that it is implicit in this statement that sin abuses not only the mind and the spirit, but even the body itself and its powers. 'Woe unto them that are mighty to drink wine, and men of strength to mingle strong drink.' People put their energy, their strength into it. There is an element of sarcasm in this 'woe'. They are no longer mighty for their country, no longer 'men of strength' for some great and noble cause. No, it all goes into this kind of thing, into pleasure, into living on drugs and standing up to drink. Body, mind, the whole of their strength, is being given to various kinds of debauchery. What a terrible abuse of the body and what an insult to human nature!

The tragedy is that while people are giving their strength to drink, to pleasure and to things of this kind, they have no conception of human beings truly functioning as they should, as men and women made by God, spirit, and soul, and body, a wonderful tri-unity, a perfect balance. They were meant to live in all these realms at the same time. How was their strength meant to be used? Our Lord summed it up by putting it like this: 'Thou shalt love the Lord thy God with all thy heart, and with all thy soul, and with all thy mind, and with all thy strength: this is the first commandment. And the second is like, namely this, Thou shalt love thy neighbour as thyself' (Mk 12:30–31). But while people are the victims of sin, and under the power of sin, they have no conception of this. They insult their mind, their soul and their body. They abuse their body by over-stimulation, and so they die at an early age, or they have frayed nerves or become the victims of psychosomatic illnesses and mental illnesses, simply because they do not know how to live.

I could illustrate this at great length. I once had the privilege of looking through the card index of the patients of a very great physician, and I found that quite frequently his diagnosis of a patient was – 'Eats too much'; 'Drinks too much'; 'Dances too much'; 'Doesn't sleep enough'. Such a patient would be working hard in his business by day, then rioting, as it were, at night, and insulting his body, and wasting his strength, not realising how to live and how to use the gifts that God had given him. Instead of using his mind, his soul, and his strength – even his physical strength – properly, he was attacking it with over-stimulation and the result was exhaustion and worry.

That brings us to the third and last principle which is taught in these two verses, and the most serious of all. Sin affects all types; no one is immune to it. It causes men and women to insult their own nature. But, thirdly, it degrades them and destroys the best and the highest in them. These things go together. 'Woe unto them that are mighty to drink wine, and men of strength to mingle strong drink: which justify the wicked for reward, and take away the righteousness of the righteous from him!' They are guilty of the last because of the others. Though they have ability and understanding, though they are in high positions, because of the degrading effect of sin in their own personal lives, their very judgement goes, everything goes. Sin always leads to degradation in every form. As it does with respect to the body, so it does, and still more so, in the highest aspects of the self.

The apostle Paul has summed up all this in famous words. He says, 'Evil communications corrupt good manners' (1 Cor 15:33). And they do! Wrong ideas will always lead to wrong practices. It may take a long time, but it always happens. I suppose that the greatest fallacy of all in the thinking of this twentieth century has been that you can have righteousness without godliness. The idea is that though you give up God, and belief in him and in the gospel, you can still maintain the righteousness taught in the gospel, you can hold on to the ethics after you have abandoned the doctrine. That has been the greatest fallacy. It began to gain currency about the middle of the Victorian era, becoming almost universal in this present century, and now we are witnessing its full effects. But you cannot have righteousness without godliness. That is the great message of the Bible. The apostle Paul puts it clearly, as we have seen, in Romans 1:18, 'For the wrath of God is revealed from heaven against all ungodliness and unrighteousness of men, who hold [down] the truth in unrighteousness.' The prophet Isaiah puts it before us in this pictorial manner. The very men to whom they looked for justice and for leadership were themselves beginning to tamper with justice. And they did so because of their own personal sin and failure. Sin always blunts the moral sense, the sense of right and wrong, and it always blunts the sense of justice.

You cannot go on sinning without your conscience being affected. What a difference there is between committing an act of sin the first time and the hundredth time. Oh, the hesitation the first time! Why? Because conscience speaks powerfully, and restrains you, warning you and saying, 'Don't! Look what happens, look at the consequences!' But if you do the act, it will be easier to repeat it the next time, still easier the next, and on and on, until at the end your conscience does not speak at all. A stage arrives, according to the apostle Paul, when your conscience has become 'seared with a hot iron' (1 Tim 4:2) and you are, as it were, a conscienceless person. Sin always corrodes the conscience, always dulls it. You cannot go on thinking wrongly, and sinning in any respect, without blunting all your moral values, your sense of right and wrong and your sense of justice.

This is the very thing, surely, that we are seeing before our eyes at the present time. I prophesy, for example, that the day is not far distant when the law courts will probably have to do away altogether with the jury system. Why? Because you cannot rely upon the men and women of the jury to bring in verdicts based upon justice. People today do not look at facts and cases in terms of right and wrong; they look at them in terms of themselves. A friend of mine was serving on a certain Grand Jury some three or four years ago and he told me what had happened. A man was up for trial on a whole series of motoring offences. The facts were put before the Court and then the jury retired.

The foreman of the jury asked, 'Well, what about it?'

To this friend of mine most of the cases were as plain as daylight – the man on trial was obviously guilty. The cases were not difficult, and there should have been no hesitation. So when the foreman of the jury put the question, my friend replied, 'Surely it is a perfectly clear case, the man is obviously guilty.' He assumed that they would all agree, and that they would soon be able to go home. But that was not what happened. The attitude of his fellow-jurymen was this: 'It might be you next time.' They said, 'Would you like a verdict of guilty if you were the man on trial?'

In other words, they were no longer thinking in terms of right and wrong, it was no longer a matter of justice, but of, 'What if it happens to me? How can I protect myself?' As Isaiah puts it, they wanted to 'justify the wicked for reward', and the reward was that they would get off when their cases came up. They were no longer looking at the crime dispassionately, objectively and honestly, but were interested parties, with ulterior motives, whose whole notion of justice had become vitiated. Why? Because they were sinners, because they knew that they would do the same thing as this man on trial. He tried to pass another car when he should not have done, or he had taken too much drink, and had been caught. Ah, what if it is you next time? What if it happens to you?

But this is not something that is confined to the ordinary

person. This is something we are witnessing on a much higher level at the present time. How frequently we read a statement on a moral question by some professor or other in a university, and the attitude is not, 'Is this right or is this wrong?' Rather, it is, 'I don't go looking into cupboards, and what I do not see I do not speak about.' That is the attitude. But it is often worse than that. Sin is being excused or explained away; the very notion of sin is being ridiculed. As we have seen, we have installed a 'new morality' worthy of the changed times in which we live. You must not continue with old ideas; as humanity evolves and changes, your ideas must change. What may have appeared wrong at one time is no longer wrong. You no longer have objective standards. Everything is in a state of flux; there is no eternal truth.

Is not this the position? Where are the guardians of morality? Where are the people who should be speaking? What of the statesmen and women? What of the leaders in the Church? What of the leaders in every department of life? You will find that they advocate 'experimental marriages' and argue that licence and even perversion in matters of sex are not always wrong, that there are times when they may be right. Love is more important than chastity; indeed, love and chastity tend to be regarded as opposites. Here is the very thing of which the prophet Isaiah was writing and on which he was pronouncing his 'woes'.

It all leads to this, that a sense of duty and of responsibility is rapidly disappearing and the idea of service has vanished. 'What can I get out of it?' 'What will pay me the most for the least effort?' Ideas of altruism and self-sacrifice are almost being despised. Everything is being excused; everything is all right. We are in a state of change; goodness is despised, integrity laughed at, and chastity and purity regarded as outmoded and old-fashioned. If you happen to be trying to live a godly and a righteous life, you may well be persecuted, laughed at, and treated with derision. 'Justify the wicked for reward, and take away the righteousness of the righteous from him!'

All this, as I said, is due to the fact that the leaders are themselves living lives of sin. Why do they attack the teaching of the Bible about sin? Because that is one of the general effects of sin upon men and women: it poisons them and makes them cynical.

'What difference does anything make?' they say. 'Give me peace; anything for a life of peace.'

Not only that, they are covering up for themselves and trying to quieten their own consciences. If your conscience is attacking you on the grounds of morality, you may think that the best way of dealing with it is to produce a 'new morality' and prove with your intellect that what is hurting you is simply a kind of hangover from a more or less undeveloped condition of the human race. So you invent a 'new morality' in order to try to quieten your own conscience. Then you take your drugs, and plunge more and more deeply into pleasure. You excuse it in others in order that you may be excused yourself. And as you go on, your highest centres are being knocked out of action and you are returning to the life of an animal.

Sometimes it is even worse than that, for the beast does not deliberately drug himself. The beast does not deliberately knock out his highest centres of understanding and of control in order to have a riot of the lower nature. He may eat poison berries without knowing what he is doing, but men and women do it deliberately. Thus human beings stand out in the whole of God's universe as the greatest fools, insulting the nature within them that has been made after the image of God, and boasting and glorying in their shame – 'Whose God is their belly, and whose glory is in their shame' (Phil 3:19). They not only do evil, but rejoice in those who do it, and encourage one another in the performance.

The Bible has nothing to say to such people except that the wrath of God is upon them. 'Woe unto them' that think and live like that. You cannot insult yourself and insult God and get away with it. If you could, God would not be God. God must deal with this; he must punish it. And he has told us that he is going to do so. He has warned us. He has pronounced his 'woes'; he has exposed sin to us. He has asked us to think and to realise these things in order that we may understand and repent.

And the business of preaching the gospel is to send out this word of invitation from God. The 'woes' are not God's last word. Realise the position, he says, and stop! 'Awake thou that sleepest, and arise from the dead, and Christ shall give thee light' (Eph 5:14). It is life you desire, is it not? It is happiness you crave, it is joy you long for. Of course it is! It is right that we should have such desires. But there is only one way they can be obtained. Any other way mocks you and deludes you; it leads you on and on and leaves you eventually in misery and despair, in unhappiness and final, utter hopelessness.

There is only one way out of all this. It is not more education; it is not further royal commissions; it is not a new department of state, nor a new Cabinet minister with special charge to deal with the problem of immorality. That will avail us nothing – nothing at all. Sin is too powerful for such expedients. It affects the greatest brain, the greatest understanding, the most stalwart person, and brings them down. It can break people physically, mentally and morally. It has been doing so throughout the running centuries and it is still doing so.

There is only one power that can deal with sin. Charles Wesley puts it like this:

> He breaks the power of cancelled sin,
> He sets the prisoner free;
> His blood can make the foulest clean,
> His blood availed for me.

That is the power of Christ, the Son of God! It is the power of his holy, sinless life; the power of his blood to cancel all your sin and iniquity; the power of his resurrection. The power of Christ through the Holy Spirit will give you a new birth, and a new nature, and a new outlook, and a new understanding – a new everything. And when you have it you will have peace; you will have joy; you will have happiness. You will no longer need drugs. You will not need to mix your cocktails. You will not need to get a kick out of artificial stimulants. You will find all in Christ, infinitely more than you can conceive. Belief in him, and receiving his life will revivify your very body. It will make a new person of you, a total personality.

And it will do this for you immediately. It will enable you to live fully while you remain in this world, and it will enable you to die triumphantly and victoriously. Then it will usher you into heaven, and the glory of God, and 'the joys that have no ending, and the love which cannot cease'. Recognise that as you are by nature, you are a victim, a slave of sin and Satan and evil. Realise also that nothing and no one but the Son of God can set you free. But he can! 'If the Son therefore shall make you free, ye shall be free indeed' (Jn 8:36).

8

Against Law and Against God

Therefore as the fire devoureth the stubble, and the flame consumeth the chaff, so their root shall be as rottenness, and their blossom shall go up as dust: because they have cast away the law of the LORD of hosts, and despised the word of the Holy One of Israel (Isaiah 5:24).

We have been considering how Isaiah's detailed exposition of the condition of his contemporaries given in chapter 5 is a message of judgement from God. But God never judges, God never punishes, without giving us his reasons. He is not capricious. He has told men and women how to live; he has laid down the conditions, and has told them very plainly what will happen if they do not fulfil these conditions. But in their folly they ignore this and live a sinful life, and so God pronounces judgement upon them. But let me emphasise once more that the object of this is to call men and women to repentance. Isaiah holds before us the offer of the gospel and it is only after we have rejected it that the punishment of God descends upon us. That is what we find in this particular chapter. As we have seen, the prophet in the first seven verses gives a general

145

summary of the whole case, then he illustrates it in six different respects, and pronounces the six 'woes' upon the Children of Israel.

Having done that, the prophet in this verse sums up the entire message again. Why is the wrath of God upon these people? Why is it that God is going to punish them? As Isaiah puts it in the next verse – 'Therefore is the anger of the LORD kindled against his people, and he hath stretched forth his hand against them, and hath smitten them.' Why? The answer is given us in this particular verse. Here, after all, is the real cause of the trouble. Here is the explanation of why the Children of Israel had been behaving in the foolish, perverted manner which we have seen as we have worked our way through the six 'woes'. This is why the wrath of God is upon them.

I call attention to all this because this is still the essential cause of all human ills and troubles. Details are important, and we have been looking at them, and have seen how contemporary they are. All the particular charges which the prophet Isaiah brought against his contemporaries are still the things that are most obvious in the world today. The details are important and we must realise them, but to stop at the details is a great mistake. The whole object of the details is to direct our attention to the principle, to the main trouble itself, and failure to realise this is fatal.

But that is exactly what is happening at the present time. The authorities are interested in details. They observe juvenile delinquency; they observe the increase in venereal diseases; they observe the increase in crimes of violence. Then, as we have said, they set up special commissions to enquire into each one and to try to discover some cure. They are dealing with the problem piecemeal; but it does not work, and never has worked. Why is this?

It is because they are only medicating symptoms, not treating the disease.

So the question we ask once more is this: Why are people capable of such unutterable folly? Why are they capable of living so foolishly? Why is the world as it is today? That is the question. We must keep on coming back to that, and we must do so because we are all in the midst of life and surrounded by problems. We see the whole world in turmoil, and the great question is: What is the matter?

Why are men and women capable of some of these things we have been looking at? Why this materialism? Why do people live for houses and for money? Why is it that they rise up early, some of them, that they may follow strong drink and just live for pleasure? Why is it that men and women 'draw iniquity with cords of vanity, and sin as it were with a cart rope'? Why are they mad on sin? Why this modern perversion, calling 'evil good, and good evil'; putting 'darkness for light, and light for darkness . . . bitter for sweet, and sweet for bitter'? Why is it that modern men and women with their world on fire are still so proud of themselves, 'wise in their own eyes, and prudent in their own sight'? Why is it that instead of competing for greatness and for the good of themselves and their country and the glory of God, they are 'mighty to drink wine, and men of strength to mingle strong drink'?

All this is very contemporary. It is a big mistake to think that the Bible is an old, old-fashioned book that does not say anything to the modern world. On the contrary, here you find wisdom for today; here you have a description of life today and the only cure for its condition. What is the explanation of why people live in this amazing and extraordinary manner? There is only one answer. It is '. . . because they have cast away the law of

the LORD of hosts, and despised the word of the Holy
One of Israel'. You may like an alternative translation:
'They have rejected the law of the LORD and *shown con-
tempt* for the words of the Holy One of Israel.'

Here is the essence of the trouble. The trouble with
men and women is not merely that they do particular
things that are wrong. The trouble with all of us by nature
is not simply that we break particular laws of God. The
real trouble is that we really reject the law of God
altogether; we dismiss it and despise it and treat it with
unutterable contempt.

That is the position at the present time, just as it was
with Israel. It is not simply that people are guilty of this
or that particular sin, it is that they do not recognise sin at
all. It is not that they are breaking particular laws of God,
but that they do not recognise the law of God and do not
recognise God himself. God and his laws are dismissed
and treated with utter contempt – that is the trouble now,
as it was in Isaiah's day. That, according to the prophet,
is what was bringing down the wrath of God upon Israel.
And it did come down. The people of Judah were
attacked by a great Chaldean army. Their army was
destroyed, their city was destroyed, and these proud
people were carried away as captives and slaves to the
land of Babylon. That was what happened, and that was
why it happened.

So, the real problem today is godlessness, the despising
of the law of God altogether, the refusal to recognise any
such category.

Now all this is as old as human civilisation; it is as old
as the human story. There is only one new element in its
present manifestation and that is that modern men and
women are trying to justify all this, trying to justify their
attitude, trying to justify it in intellectual terms. They are

writing books about it and some of them are called religious and others philosophical. They speak about it on the television and on the radio. In this way they are asserting their liberty. They are trying to show that they have shaken off the chains of religion and got rid of 'the dope of the people', and that they have now found something greater, something superior, something which really makes them grown up.

That is the one new feature about this present rejection of God and his laws – that it presents itself to us as a great advance, as something noble and wonderful. It claims to be offering us emancipation and liberty. That is what makes it so serious. There is always hope for sinners who know they are sinners. If you know that you are a sinner the door of heaven is open to you. However deeply men and women may have sinned, as long as they know it, as long as they feel it, and as long as they regret it, there is everlasting hope for them and the Christian gospel has a glorious message to offer them. But if they do not even recognise the fact of sin, if they are proud of the life they are living, and try to justify it intellectually, then, while they remain in that condition, there is no hope whatsoever for them. To remain like that is final hopelessness, and they are completely lost until they are convicted and acknowledge their transgression.

That is the position confronting us today; and it is upon this that God pronounces his 'woe'. It is because 'they have cast away the law of the LORD of hosts, and despised' – treated with contempt – 'the word of the Holy One of Israel'.

This is, obviously, a most serious matter, the kind of thing which brings down the wrath of God upon individuals, upon communities and upon countries. We must therefore examine it, and as we proceed to do so, let me

make one thing quite clear, lest there be any misunderstanding. What I am talking about is the kind of
person who rejects the law of God and the words of the
Holy One of Israel. I am not speaking about people who
are merely reacting against the codes of society. I am not
dealing with people who are simply reacting against, and
objecting to, a superficial morality, nor am I dealing with
people who object to mere respectability.

I want to make this very plain. There is a reaction in the
present generation against what we may well call Victorianism – and I am the last man in the world to defend
that. Indeed, I would lay claim to being one of its most
constant critics. I have no use for Victorianism – that age
in which it was the thing to do to go to a place of worship
because you would probably get a better job if you did,
and it was the respectable thing to do. I am not here to
defend that. I am not interested in 'religion'; neither is it
my business to preach morality as such. I am not a Christian preacher in order to try to help the Government to
maintain law and order, or because I am interested in the
political welfare of this country; that is not my object. So
if you are merely objecting to a social code, or a superficial easy morality, or a self-righteous respectability, I am
with you. I am on your side. I am against it as much as
you are. I do not defend sham and pretence and mere
hypocrisy.

I know that modern men and women have reacted violently against all that. I was brought up in that kind of
atmosphere; there was more of it at the beginning of the
century than there is today. I remember the beginning of
the reaction against late Victorian and Edwardian respectable religion, and I was one of the people who objected to
it, and I still do. I am forty years older but I still say what
I said then. Religion is often the greatest enemy of

Christianity. Respectability is the antithesis of true Christian living. You can say as much as you like against sham and pretence and hypocrisy. I will say 'Amen' to it; I will applaud; I will say 'Quite right!' But the trouble is that modern men and women, in reacting against all that, have gone so far as to reject 'the law of God and the words of the Most High'.

Now let us be fair. I have a great sympathy with those who react. Let me give you a simple illustration of what I mean. Look at the poor people in Russia who believe in atheistic communism. Why are they in that position? There is no difficulty about answering that question. Their only conception of Christianity was what they saw in the Russian Orthodox Church, and especially in the life of a man like Rasputin, who had such terrible power over the last Czar of Russia, and particularly over his wife. That was the Russian people's conception of Christianity. They said that they did not want it, because it was so horrible; so they have gone right away from it and have become atheists.

And that is the tragedy. They were right in objecting to the horror of Rasputin, but they did not realise that that was a perversion of Christianity, and in their blindness and ignorance they rejected the whole of Christianity and every belief in God.

So let us be quite clear as to what we are considering. We are considering men and women who reject the law of God, and God himself, and every word that comes from the Most High. And that is the position of the vast majority of people. They hate God and his laws and true Christianity. They are violent about it and are bitterly opposed to it. This is almost incredible, but it is a fact; and, at the same time, they justify their 'new morality', which is their conception of morality without God. How, then, have they ever got into such a condition?

Let us analyse it in terms of what we are told here by Isaiah. The first explanation is that they are guilty of a complete misunderstanding of the law. 'They have cast away the law of the LORD of hosts' because they have a fundamental misconception of it. They have a feeling that the law is not for our good and for our well-being, but that it is something which is against us. They want to get rid of this law of the Lord because they feel that it has been the enemy.

They rebel against the law of God for three main reasons. First, they hate it because they feel that it is opposed to happiness. They want happiness, and they say that nothing has so stood between men and women and happiness as this law. They say that it makes people feel that they are miserable sinners. It also says 'No' to everything they want to do. It causes people to crucify their own natural powers. It makes them live unnatural lives and makes them regard as wrong that which is essentially right. And so, they say, it leads to perpetual misery. So they object to the law of the Lord and cast it on one side. They regard it as entirely negative and purely restrictive. To quote Milton, they regard it as something that leads a person 'to scorn delights, and live laborious days'.

But here the question that arises is: What is happiness? We all desire it. There is nothing wrong in that: we are meant to be happy. God made us and intended us to be happy. But the tragedy of the modern position is that it regards happiness as experience only. You can find this in the literature, in the drama, in all the things we have been mentioning. This is the test of happiness – experience, and especially 'the experience of the moment'. The present moment! Nothing else matters but that. You shut out everything else; you do not consider anything but the present experience; and that is what accounts for much of the trouble today and so much of the calamity.

Such a definition of happiness is too small and much too narrow. Happiness must be defined in terms of the total person; but it is defined now in terms of certain particular experiences only. The argument is that we cannot be really happy unless we are given liberty here and now. That is the idea of happiness – the gratification of my desire at this moment; nothing else is considered. The whole person – the mind, the soul, the conscience – is not considered; tomorrow is not considered; consequences are not considered.

The result is, of course, quite inevitable. If you start out with a false conception of happiness, you are never going to find it; and the modern man or woman who is living for pleasure and for happiness is not finding it. Such people are throwing away the law of the Lord. They say, 'We cannot be happy while this idea of law, this incubus of morality, is upon us; let us get rid of that and then we shall be happy.'

But they are not happy. Why not? Because each person has a conscience. They do not believe in conscience, but it is there, and they cannot get rid of it. You cannot get rid of remorse, you cannot abolish a sense of shame: they are there. 'The experience of the moment! This is living! This is happiness!' Is it? What about the next day? There are certain laws of life. The Bible has told us from the beginning that 'the way of transgressors is hard' (Prov 13:15). If you break the laws of God, you will have to suffer. There is a law of life and of being and of happiness. The facts are proving that the modern rebellion against God's law and the false quest for happiness are not bringing happiness.

On what grounds do I say that? I suggest that the

divorce figures are proving it to the very hilt. I read recently that one out of every two marriages in Los Angeles ends in divorce. And that is the place where they believe in 'liberty', is it not? That is where they live for happiness. Los Angeles! Hollywood! That is life! But here is the result – one out of two marriages dissolved! They have thrown out the law of God, but have they found happiness? And it does not end, unfortunately, with divorce – there is the drug-taking, the drink, always the craving for some fresh experience. If people are so happy, why do they have to do these things? They are not happy – and it is because their whole notion of happiness is wrong. It is too small. They do not start by looking at human beings and considering what they are, and realising that before they can be happy, every part of them must be satisfied. They just want the present experience, the immediate enjoyment.

The tragedy is that men and women can still be so foolish as to believe that they can find happiness along those particular lines. It has been tried so often before. Let me give you one example which is perhaps one of the most dramatic and striking – the case of the great Christian teacher, St Augustine. He had tried it all, away back towards the end of the fourth century. Here was this man with all his genius, his brilliant philosophy. He was not a Christian but he was trying to find happiness and he had tried in the way in which people are trying to find happiness now. He could not find it. He tried it very thoroughly. There is nothing new about keeping a mistress. It is as old as human nature. He had tried it all, but his great brain was not satisfied, he felt a lack and he went on trying to find happiness. Then came that dramatic moment when he made his great confession:

Thou hast made us for thyself
And our hearts are restless
Until they find their rest in thee.

Secondly, people rebel against the law because they regard it as being the opposite of liberty. This, of course, is the great claim – that religion holds you back, tells you not to do this or that, does not let you express yourself. 'We want liberty,' they say. 'We want freedom.' This is so well known to all of us. Every one of us has been through it. As an adolescent you looked forward to the day when you would no longer be forced to go to Sunday school; when you would be an adult and decide for yourself what to do; when you would be free and get away from church and chapel, and God and religion, and really live your own life in freedom! Such young people put law and liberty over against one another – and this is another tragic error because the question that arises now is: What is liberty? And the modern idea of liberty is licence: do what you like; every man for himself; have a good time; let nothing restrain you; do not worry about other people. If you want something – well, it's yours. Take it and don't think of anybody else!

But that is licence, not liberty. And again, the tragedy of it all is that it does not lead to liberty. You can kick over the traces, you can push the law of God out through the door, you can spit upon the sanctities and 'despise the words of the Holy One of Israel' but do not imagine for a moment that this is the way to get liberty, because it is not. Let me tell you why. Our Lord has put it in a great statement which you will find in the eighth chapter of John's Gospel. When he was speaking one day, some people seemed to believe in him and our Lord looked at them and said, 'If ye continue in my word, then are ye my disciples indeed; and ye shall know the truth, and the truth shall make you free.'

But they did not like that. Turning on him, they said, 'We be Abraham's seed, and were never in bondage to any man: how sayest thou, Ye shall be made free?'

And our Lord answered, 'Verily, verily, I say unto you, Whosoever committeth sin is the servant [the slave] of sin' (Jn 8:31–34).

You can get rid of law but you do not get liberty. No, you become the slave of sin. Think of men and women who have defied the name of God and blasphemed it and thrown all the laws right out. Have they got liberty? Poor slaves! They are slaves to sex and to drink and to various other things that grip them and manipulate them; slaves to their profession; slaves to jealousy and pride. Look at the life of society. They are, they say, too intelligent to believe in God, but look at the miserable slavery of this polite life in society. They are jealous of one another's dress and appearance and car and house and yacht, and this and that. It is sheer slavery! No, no! 'Whosoever committeth sin is the servant of sin.' You do not find liberty, you do not find happiness, by throwing the law out of the window.

Let me quote you some excellent words by Field Marshal Lord Slim which I was reading recently. I think this is a very profound summing up of the whole of this discussion. 'You can have discipline,' he says, 'without liberty, but you cannot have liberty without discipline.' Why not? For this reason: you are not really free until you are in the right relationship with everybody else. You get what you want but the other man will do so also, and you will feel that he is holding you down; you will not be free. There is no such thing as liberty without discipline, and the tragedy of today is that men and women are convinced that there is. They think the way to be free is to break and to throw out the law of God. They know nothing about what James called 'the perfect law of liberty', or, as a phrase in the Prayer Book puts it: 'whose service is perfect freedom'. They are ignorant of that. Their whole notion of liberty has gone astray.

But thirdly, they regard law as being the opposite of love, and this is the favourite of all. They believe in 'love'. Professor Carstairs, a Reith lecturer, said that the whole trouble is due to the fact that the Church has put chastity before love. But love is the thing! So he goes on to advocate experimental marriage and so on. Love, people say, is the opposite of law. The Church has been preaching law and everybody has been miserable. What we need is love! So they contrast that with the teaching of the apostle Paul, of whom they are so woefully ignorant, and the great Reith lecturer showed profound and colossal ignorance of Paul's whole teaching – Paul the misogynist, he said, the man who is against women!

What utter rubbish it is! Why do they not *read* the apostle Paul? To contrast him with the teaching of the Lord Jesus Christ is blasphemy. No one ever honoured the Lord Jesus Christ more than the apostle Paul. There is no contradiction whatsoever, it is precisely the same teaching. But in these terms they put love against law, law against love.

So the question we must ask here is: What is love? And I suppose of all questions that modern men and women ought to consider, this is one of the first. We are living in a sex-ridden and media-ridden generation. That is where the contemporary notion of love comes from. It is nothing but lust, living like an animal, letting yourself go – that is thought to be love. What else? Well, some vague well-wishing and so on. And, of course, the law of God is against that, and rightly so. It is against lust and against this vague, general, meaningless talk. The law of God is strong and powerful; it is an expression of the love of God. It is not opposed to love.

The apostle Paul says, 'Love worketh no ill to his neighbour' (Rom 13:10). The essence of the law of God, he says, is this: 'Thou shalt love thy neighbour as thyself . . . love is the fulfilling of the law' (vv. 9–10). Far from being the antithesis of law, love carries out the law; and love is strong; it is noble; it is pure; it is clean and upright. Our Lord Jesus Christ was the very incarnation of God's love. He was perfect love and he says, 'Think not that I am come to destroy the law, or the prophets: I am not come to destroy, but to fulfil' (Mt 5:17). It is tragic how men and women today reject the law of God because they do not understand it, because they have a complete misconception with regard to its meaning.

The second cause of this rebellion against and rejection of the law of God is this: it is a complete misunderstanding of the true nature of men and women. 'Because they have cast away the law of the LORD of hosts, and despised the word of the Holy One of Israel.' Why do they do that? It is because they do not understand the law, yes; but still more tragic, in trying to exalt themselves, people are debasing themselves and showing that the real trouble is that they do not understand themselves and their own true nature. They think that law is against them, against their nature and an insult to them. They say, 'Why must I have law? Why must I be kept down? Why can't I be allowed to express myself?' So the cult is that of self-expression.

But here the question is: What, then, is man or woman? What is the modern view? If people say, 'I do not like law because it is an insult to me' – then we are entitled to ask,

'Well, who are you? What are you?' And they have no answer. This is one of the most tragic things of all. Here is one of the definitions of man today: he is, we are told, a 'bundle of sensations'! There is no such thing as 'I' or 'me'. I am told that 'I' am nothing but this 'bundle of sensations'. There are all sorts of impulses and instincts and desires within me – sensations – and as I react to others and to the world, I get more sensations. I am what I am momentarily. I am, at this moment, aware of certain sensations, some of pleasure, some of pain, some of agreement, some of disagreement and so on; but I am nothing but this momentary sensation.

This is a very serious matter. Modern men and women have ceased to believe in God and in God's law, so what is the favourite philosophy today? It is what is called the existentialist view of humanity, existentialism. It is extremely popular. You find it in books, plays and films. What does it tell us about who I am? Well let me give you some quotations. I am 'a mere nucleus of conscious experience in the space-time stream'. Life is a space-time stream, it is moving on and I am just a sort of little nucleus of experience in it.

Here is another definition. *Sum cogitens*, which means, I am a thought centre. I am capable of thinking, and I think certain thoughts. That is really all I can know about myself.

Then listen to another: 'We are finite in an infinite process, and we become real by accepting this fact instead of deluding ourselves by the false stability of conceptual thinking.' So what am I? I am a finite being in some infinite process that is carrying me on. There was life before I came; there is life now; there will be life after me. Here is an infinite process. I know no beginning and no end to it. But I am finite. I was not always here; I shall not always be here. And the way to become real is to accept this fact, instead of deluding myself by believing in God and in salvation.

Or let me give you another definition – and I am doing this very deliberately. It is because they believe this kind of thing about themselves that people reject the law of God and spit upon the word of the Holy One of Israel. Take a great French writer – I say great, because he is a great writer, but he is an unbeliever, an infidel – Jean-Paul Sartre. This is his teaching. He says he has accepted complete atheism and complete free will, and he is prepared to draw the consequences from those two propositions. Humanity, he says, must make its vital choices without any sure premises from which to reason. I do not know anything, I cannot be certain of anything, but I must make my choices. I must live, and living means making choices.

'So,' I say, 'on what grounds can I decide?'

Sartre replies: We are thrown into the world, we know not how, and left free to make ourselves by our choices. But we have no rules, no principles, no truth, by which to choose. Our situation, Sartre says, is absurd, because our concept of ourselves, our essence, is always in front of what we are at the present. He says: I am never what I want to be; I am never what I know I ought to be. I am always moving, but I never get there, and that is why our whole position is absurd.

And what does it all end in? Well, according to Sartre it ends in despair and nausea, a perpetual feeling of sickness. And the modern age is sick of life, hence all the literature and the drama and the architecture and everything else I have spoken about. It is a sick age! It is a nausea! Men and women are sick and tired; they do not know where they are. It is all too big for them and yet they claim they understand. They admit they have no grounds at all on which to reason but they have to make vital choices. That is their view of themselves, and it is because of this that they reject the law of God.

But furthermore, they believe that they are still capable of deciding; they still think they can decide what is best for them. But how can they? Every opinion differs, and the moment you get these differing opinions there are clashes and you cannot have harmony or a good life. Not only that, people, as they are by nature, are selfish and self-centred; they are self-justifying and controlled by desire. But they still think that they are capable of making right decisions, and, still more monstrous and ridiculous, they think that men and women are capable of carrying out their decisions after they have arrived at them. They still say that human beings do not need God; they can make their own world and they can make it into something wonderful.

What is the answer? It is given once and for ever in the epistle to the Romans, in chapter 7: 'To will is present with me; but how to perform that which is good I find not. For the good that I would I do not: but the evil which I would not, that I do' (Rom 7:18–19). And that is true of every man and woman. There is a perpetual struggle and they cannot do it; yet they say they can. But men and women are a mass of contradictions. From the very dawn of civilisation they have been admitting that in practice they cannot govern themselves and they cannot do what they know to be right.

Even in the most primitive tribes there are tribal customs and taboos, rules and regulations. Why is this? It is because communal life is impossible apart from that. Let every man and woman do what they like and you get nothing but chaos. Even modern humanists have to recognise that in practice you have got to have some limits, that you must have some rules. They recognise that certain things are wrong. But by not believing in anarchy they grant the whole principle: you must have law. And indeed this is obvious on the international level. Why do we need the United Nations Organisation? Why are world leaders thinking in terms of some international parliament, or peace force? It is because people must be kept in order and cannot do that themselves, either individually or as national groups.

And all this is because, as the Bible puts it, men and women are fallen creatures; they are evil. If they were good, they would not need law. Laws are not made for the righteous but for the unrighteous, and the whole of humanity is unrighteous. They are fallen creatures who have gone astray; they are lost; they are creatures of lust and desire; they do not live according to their brains, though they try to persuade themselves that they do. Their greatest need is wisdom; they need knowledge; they need control and power.

This has all been gone through so often. Go back to ancient Greece before the birth of Jesus Christ. In Athens there was, at one and the same time, the brilliant teaching of the philosophers and, as the apostle Paul discovered, an altar to the Unknown God (Acts 17). They could not find God so they had to postulate him, and they built an altar to him and proceeded to worship him in ignorance. That is the final admission that human beings are incapable of ordering their own lives. They cannot get on without law; they cannot get on without God. And yet in their folly they think they can and so they despise the law of God.

The last point is this: this rejection of law at the present time is not only due to a misunderstanding of law and a misunderstanding of human nature, supremely it is based upon an utter ignorance of God, '. . . because they have cast away the law of the LORD of hosts, and despised the word of the Holy One of Israel.' The prophet Isaiah brings out the nature of God by describing him in those two different ways – 'The LORD of hosts', and 'The Holy One of Israel'. Oh, this is the tragedy of modern men and women; they think that God is against them, that he is some monster who is opposed to them and is keeping them down and in subjection. That is the whole tragedy; it was the first sin.

But still worse, those who reject the law of God hate above everything else the holiness of God. That is a terrible thing, but it is true. People are ready to believe in a God of love but they hate the idea of a holy God. 'The Holy One of Israel!' They do not like holiness; they feel it is against them and their best interests, it is against what they want to do. When God says, 'Because I am God, thou shalt not,' they hate him and there is no more terrible indictment of modern people than their hatred of the holiness of God.

And in the same way, in their ignorance they defy the power of God, 'because they have cast away the law of the LORD of Hosts', the God who commands the sun and the moon and the stars, the God who reigns over all, who made everything and who sustains everything – the Lord God Jehovah! Lord of Hosts! Infinite, absolute in power! And they stand up and defy him; they reject his holy law and despise his most holy words. They do not realise that they are in the hands of God, that God is everywhere and that he cannot be escaped. They do not realise that 'it is a fearful thing to fall into the hands of the living God' (Heb 10:31). They do not know that with all their cleverness they have got to die and meet God. Do what they will, they cannot escape it or avoid it. 'The Holy One of

Israel!' 'The LORD God of hosts!' That is the explanation of the tragedy of modern men and women.

What do they need? Well, it is plain, is it not? They need to know the truth about God – that God *is*, that he is holy and righteous and all-powerful. They need to know God as their Maker and Creator, the one who has given them life and being in order that they might live to his glory and enjoy him for ever. They need to know that.

They need to know also the truth about themselves, that they are not animals, nor a 'bundle of sensations'. They need to know, rather, that they are created in the image and likeness of God (Gen 1:26), that they have a mind and understanding, a soul and a spirit, that they are bigger than the world and life and all experience, that they are living souls.

Furthermore, they need to know, therefore, the truth about life and how to live it. They need to know that their happiness is based upon one thing only and that is the knowledge of God and the keeping of God's holy law. They need to know that if they only do that, they will find the happiness, the liberty, and the love that they are longing for and looking for. Our Lord taught, 'Thou shalt love thy neighbour as thyself,' and if only we all loved our neighbour as we love ourselves, then the world would be perfect and we would never take advantage of anybody. I would never do harm to another to satisfy my lust; I would have respect for the other; I would have love for the other and consider the other as I consider myself. So also would nations. There would be perfect peace if only we loved our neighbour as ourselves.

But what will enable me to do that? Our Lord, as we have seen, has given us the answer. There is only one way in which I will ever come to love my neighbour as myself and it is this: 'Thou shalt love the Lord thy God with all thy heart, and with all thy soul, and with all thy mind, and with all thy strength: this is the first commandment. And the second is like, namely this, Thou shalt love thy neighbour as thyself' (Mk 12:30–31). And you will never know yourself, or love yourself properly, until you know God and are living for him and his glory. Once you do that, you are right with your neighbour also, and you love your neighbour as yourself. But none of us does that, none of us can do that, and because we fail, we say, 'It is this religion, this law of God that is upsetting everything.' But it is the other way round – get right with God, begin to obey him and all your problems will be solved.

And this is the wonderful message of the Christian gospel. It is because we cannot do it and do not even want to do it that 'God so loved the world, that he gave his only begotten Son, that whosoever believeth in him should not perish, but have everlasting life' (Jn 3:16). God saw us in our misery, in our slavery and lovelessness, and in his compassion he sent his Son from heaven down into this world, even to die upon a cross, in order to set us free. So when our Lord, as we saw earlier, said, 'Whosoever committeth sin is the servant of sin,' he went on to say this: 'If the Son therefore shall make you free, ye shall be free indeed' (Jn 8:34, 36). Free from lust, free from all the things that enchain you, free in the freedom that God alone can give.

Let me put it to you, then, in the words of the apostle Paul. There he was, trying to live a righteous life and failing, and at last in his utter agony and failure he cried out, 'O wretched man that I am! who shall deliver me from the body of this death?' – this contradiction that I am. And the answer comes, 'I thank God through Jesus Christ our Lord' (Rom 7:24–25). 'The law of the Spirit of life in Christ Jesus hath made me free from the law of sin and death' (Rom 8:2). I am a free man! So Paul was able to say with the psalmist, 'O how I love thy law!' (Ps 119:97). 'I delight to do thy will, O my God' (Ps 40:8).

There is only one way to find happiness and liberty; there is only one way to find love. Here is a man who has seen it and this is how he prays:

> My will is not my own
> Till Thou hast made it Thine;
> If it would reach the monarch's throne
> It must its crown resign.
>
> *George Matheson*

Do not believe the lie of the devil that to be a Christian is to be miserable, to be a slave and to lack love. No, this is liberty, this is life, this is joy and this is peace. 'If the Son shall make you free, ye shall be free indeed.'

9

The Verdict

Therefore is the anger of the LORD kindled against his people, and he hath stretched forth his hand against them, and hath smitten them: and the hills did tremble, and their carcases were torn in the midst of the streets. For all this his anger is not turned away, but his hand is stretched out still (Isaiah 5:25).

Here in this verse, the prophet is pronouncing his verdict. God had given him this message to Israel because things were beginning to go wrong. There were false prophets – there are always false prophets. We are told that they were the people who always came and 'healed the hurt of the daughter of my people slightly, saying, Peace, peace; when there is no peace' (Jer 8:11). That is always the trouble with false prophets. They are out to please, to be popular, and they know that people like to be told, 'Peace, peace.' People like to be told that everything is all right. 'Don't get worried. Don't get anxious. Don't get frightened. There is something wrong but it's not very serious, it can soon be put right. Peace, peace . . . .' And they were there in their numbers, addressing the Children of Israel.

But the true prophet is called by God, and his is not a message of 'Peace, peace'. He does not merely look at the surface conditions and make a superficial diagnosis, nor is he concerned merely with medicating symptoms. He is concerned about the truth, he really wants to help, and he knows that you have got to be cruel to be kind. He tells the truth, and that is what we have in this chapter 5. 'All these things are coming upon you,' says the prophet, 'because you have not conducted yourselves as the people of God.' That is the meaning, as we saw, of that poem, that parable, in the first seven verses.

Then Isaiah goes through the particular sins and transgressions of which the people were guilty, and, as we have just seen, he sums it up in the final charge against the Children of Israel, that 'they have cast away the law of the LORD of hosts, and despised the word of the Holy One of Israel'. That is the charge, and here now is the verdict on that charge: 'Therefore is the anger of the LORD kindled against his people, and he hath stretched forth his hand against them, and hath smitten them.' It has been severe, and it is not finished; even this is not the end. '. . . but his hand is stretched out still.' Why? Because they will not repent.

So let us look at this great message together. You notice that it reminds us of what is, of course, the most prominent word in the entire chapter, the word 'woe'. We have had six woes pronounced, and here it is summed up in the word 'anger' or 'wrath'.

After that, the remainder of the chapter is purely descriptive. Verses 26 to the end are but a detailed description of the kind of punishment that God is going to send upon the people of Judah. So this verse is really the end of our consideration of this chapter.

As I call your attention to this verse, I am fully aware

of the fact that there is no aspect of the biblical message that so annoys modern men and women as the whole notion of the wrath of God, of God as one who punishes sin and iniquity. There is no part, no element in the biblical teaching, to which people take such a rooted and violent objection as this particular truth.

Now of course it is not surprising that people should find this objectionable. Particularly, it is not surprising that it should be objectionable to the kind of person we were considering when we were dealing with those who object to the whole notion of law, the whole notion, ultimately, of morality, indeed, the whole teaching about God. It is not surprising that they should object to this doctrine of the wrath of God, they would be inconsistent if they did not. I want to grant that their position is, at any rate, coherent and logical. If you do not believe in law, then I do not expect you to believe in the doctrine of the anger of God and God's punishment of sin. The one follows inevitably from the other.

So the objection to this doctrine is found among those who are not Christians and who are outside the Church. They object to this above everything else. They say, 'We understand the idea of the love of God, but this notion of anger and wrath and God's hand stretched out – it is impossible.' 'The natural man', as the Bible calls such people, those who do not claim to be Christians, resent this doctrine, and they have always done so. But, alas, the objection is not confined to people who are outside the Church. At the present time there are many inside the Church who object to the doctrine quite as much as those on the outside. There are those who take what they call a 'liberal' view of the Scriptures and they abominate this doctrine of the wrath of God.

Now I want in particular to deal with the second group

but, of course, at the same time I do trust that I shall also be dealing, at any rate in a measure, with the case of those who are outside the Church. I pay tribute, let me repeat, to those who are outside – at any rate they are consistent and logical. But I cannot pay any tribute to those inside the Church who deny the doctrine of the wrath of God. They are really in an indefensible position, as I hope to show you; there is no consistency about them at all. At least let us have people who are consistent, who have a position, not people who are half in and half out, and who take some and leave the rest. It is either all or nothing when you come to this biblical doctrine.

This is a vital matter, looked at not only from the standpoint of the Christian message and the Christian Church, but also from a more general political and social standpoint. If it were my business to do so, I do not think I should have much difficulty in demonstrating that quite a number of our present-day problems – political, social problems, I mean – really derive from this rooted objection to the whole notion of discipline, of order, of law, of righteousness, of justice, of punishment and of retribution. I think that this objection to these principles accounts in a very large measure for the breakdown of discipline in home life and may very well be at the root of much of the modern problem of juvenile delinquency.

But again, let us be fair, let us be honest. I know that we are suffering in this century from a reaction against what I have referred to as Victorianism. Far be it from me to attempt to defend the Victorian type of father, that tyrant, but the world has reacted violently against that, and its reaction, of course, like all reactions, has gone too far. It has reached a point of lawlessness, and the modern father, in his desire not to be like the stern, harsh, unloving Victorian father, has become so easy-going and indulgent that he does not believe in discipline at all. And the result is what is witnessed so often, unfortunately, in home life and in the life of the family, in schools and in the general lack of decent behaviour among young people.

And then another result – I just mention this in passing – is our whole attitude towards prisons and what should happen in a prison. What is the purpose of sending someone to prison? Now the idea today is that it is not to punish the offender, we do not believe in retribution. The object of the prison, we are told, is reformation, and you are familiar with some of the details to which this has led; the whole question, for instance, as to whether there is such a thing as sin is in the balance at the moment.

Indeed, the whole question as to whether there is such a thing as crime also seems to be in the balance. For some people there will soon be no criminals, we shall all be 'ill' in some shape or form! Crime becomes a medical, not a legal, problem, and then you do not punish people but you treat them. So you call in your psychotherapists and there is no punishment. I do think it is time that we began to examine this whole matter much more seriously, because our modern efforts do not seem to be reaping very good results. But there it is – this fundamental objection to the whole idea of law and the application of law, especially in punishment, is one to which modern thought has a very violent and rooted objection.

What, then, is the difficulty? Why is there this objection? And, particularly, why is there this objection among people who call themselves Christian? It seems to me that there are two obvious answers. The first is that people do not submit themselves to the revelation of the Bible. Now this is quite basic. In the last analysis there are only two positions open to both those inside and outside the Church: either to submit to the revelation and the teaching of the Bible or else to refuse. As far as I am concerned, that is the only classification that matters. Nothing else really matters from the standpoint of the person who believes the Bible.

Now the trouble with these people who say they are Christians and yet do not believe in punishment is that they accept the Bible in some things but not in others. They say they do not believe in this because they cannot reconcile it with the idea of God as a God of love, and the people outside say the same thing. They say, 'But it is unthinkable that God should have wrath and anger, or that he ever stretched forth his hand in punishment.' They say, 'Such a God is not a God of love, and I could not possibly believe in him.' Even people inside the Church say that.

Their trouble is that their notion of God is not derived from the Bible, but is what *they* think of God, what *they* think of love. They start with their own ideas and then, because the Bible does not agree, they reject the Bible. They are the judges, they are the standard, they have rejected the whole category of revelation and we shall see the significance of that.

But the second reason for this position is this – and to me this is the most important reason, and at the same time a very fascinating one! These people fail to see the wholeness of the biblical message. Now many different doctrines are taught in the Bible, but the glory of the Bible is that they are all one, they are all facets of one great, central, unified truth. That alone, as far as I am concerned, would be more than enough to make me believe that the Bible is the word of God. Here is a great book which consists of sixty-six different books incorporated into the one, written at different times, by different people, with centuries between them, and yet they are all saying the same thing.

There is one great message from Genesis to Revelation, one central theme. Everything is brought into a magnificent unity. There is a wholeness which is superb and divine, and the trouble with these people is that they have never seen that. They look at doctrines in isolation, and because they look at them like that, because they concentrate on the particulars and miss the whole, they cannot even understand the particular. Thus they tend to go wrong at every point.

If you leave out this doctrine of the wrath of God, the whole biblical doctrine of salvation collapses. If I did not believe in the doctrine of the wrath of God, I would not understand the death of Christ upon the cross, it would be meaningless to me. You cannot pick and choose with this; you either take it all or you take none. That is why I must emphasise again that the people who seem to me to be doing the greatest harm to the Christian cause are muddled Christians, not the people who are right outside the Church. They miss the wholeness, the oneness, the unity, the grandeur. They do not see how each doctrine fits into the other! They do not understand that if you take out one, you have destroyed everything.

So people who do not believe in the doctrine of the wrath of God never have a right view of the cross. Their view of the cross is something sentimental, something superficial. It is bound to be so, because they have not got hold of the essential key to the understanding of the glory of the cross.

So let us look at that momentous event that happened on the first Good Friday, when Jesus of Nazareth was crucified on Calvary between the two thieves. He had ridden into Jerusalem on 'the foal of an ass', and the people had thrown down their clothes, cut down the palm branches and strewn them on the road, and shouted out,

'Hosanna; Blessed is he that cometh in the name of the Lord' (Mk 11:9). But he was going to death, to crucifixion; he was going to shame, ignominy, scorn and incredible suffering.

What is it all about? Now this is a matter of history. Jesus of Nazareth belongs to history. That Palm Sunday actually occurred.[1] It is not a story; it is a fact that took place. And the great matter that should be concerning us is this: Who is this Jesus? What was he doing there, this person riding on a donkey? Why, especially, did he ever arrive at that cross? Has all this got a meaning? And my suggestion to you is that you will never understand it unless you understand the biblical teaching concerning the wrath of God and his anger upon sin.

Why, then, is this essential? I want to give you three answers. The first is that the doctrine of the wrath of God is absolutely essential to an understanding of the truth about God himself. Here, of course, is the primary proposition. It is all a matter of knowing God. What is the truth about God? That is what Christianity is concerned about. This idea that Christianity is just something that gives me a nice feeling, or makes me forget my troubles, that it is some sort of opiate or anodyne, is an absolute travesty. I know it has often been presented like that – 'Come to Jesus and you will get this, that and the other.' But that is not biblical Christianity. Biblical Christianity is this: God and my relationship to him!

But who is God? What is God? That is the fundamental question. What do I know about God? Nay more, how can I know anything about him? You see, whether or not you believe in the wrath of God depends upon your view

---

[1] This sermon was preached on Palm Sunday 1964.

of God, but from where do you get that view? And here is the point at which so many go astray. 'Canst thou by searching find out God?' (Job 11:7). Well, the apostle Paul, a brilliant and a learned man, has told us that 'the world by wisdom' – by which he meant philosophy – 'knew not God' (1 Cor 1:21). Oh yes, the philosophers had been feeling after him, there is no question about that; those mighty men had grappled with this problem. They were aware of the complexity of the problem of life and they were trying to understand it. They were asking fundamental questions. But the trouble was that they could not arrive at an answer. Can a man by searching find out God? And the answer is, 'No.'

I sometimes think that there is nothing more interesting in the whole of the New Testament than the story in Acts 17. It is the story of the visit paid by the apostle Paul to the famous city of Athens. There is no question but that he had gone there on holiday. He had been treated badly at Thessalonica and at Berea, so his friends had taken him down to the sea and he had gone to Athens in order to have a rest. But he was unable to rest, he had to start speaking because, as he said to the Athenian people, 'I perceive that in all things you are too superstitious [too religious].'

What had made Paul come to that conclusion? Well, he had found the famous city of Athens, the great centre of the philosophers, the home and the seat of philosophy, he had found it cluttered up with temples and altars to various idols. And, most interesting of all, among those altars he had found one with this inscription on it – 'To the Unknown God'.

That was a tremendous confession. Athens had seen philosophy at its best, and the great flowering period of philosophy, the time of the real 'masters', had already come and gone, remember, when this happened. But here, in spite of that teaching, they had an 'Unknown God'! There was a power outside, they believed, bigger, greater than man and his mind, his thinking and his understanding; there were powers influencing this world; there were 'gods'. So with their philosophy they had too much 'religion' as it were, but they were seeking after him and they could not find him. 'The world by wisdom knew not God', and it still cannot know God by wisdom.

And the reason for that is the very character and being of God. If I could find God it would mean that I was bigger than God. If God is an object that I can examine and dissect, then I am bigger than he. But God, by definition, is beyond; he is absolute; he is eternal.

And so the biblical teaching is that men and women can ultimately know nothing about God unless God chooses to reveal himself. Oh yes, I grant you that by studying nature and creation you can arrive at a belief in a Creator. That is what Sir James Jeans arrived at – there must be a great Mind behind the universe. He said that his scientific knowledge led him to that conclusion. But that only brings you to the knowledge of God as very powerful, to God as Creator. That is the argument of the apostle Paul in the first chapter of the epistle to the Romans. It can bring you to that, but that is not a knowledge of God. I want to know God as he is; I want to know God who is personal; I want to know the attributes of God's character. And that is where I cannot succeed; that is where no one can succeed or has ever succeeded – the mystery of God! The *mysterium tremendum* as someone called it, and that is what it is. It is the ultimate – God! We are shut in to revelation. We know nothing about God except what he has been pleased to reveal to us.

And, thank God, he has been pleased to give us that

revelation! That is the great message of the Bible. It is a great fallacy to think and to say that the Bible is the record of man's search for God. It is the exact opposite. It is the record of man's failure, and of God graciously revealing himself and his purpose for the world. It is the record of revelation not of discovery. These are antitheses, absolute opposites.

So God has given us this revelation. He gave it to Adam and Eve and to Cain, their son. He gave a revelation of himself to the people before the Flood and to the people who built the Tower of Babel, in their cleverness and in their attempt to reach the heavens. He gave a revelation in the Ten Commandments which he gave to Moses, and in the moral law. He gave the message to the prophets. Indeed, the whole of the Old Testament is nothing, in a sense, but a great record of God's revelation of himself.

And what does he teach? It is this: 'I am the Lord thy God! I am a holy God!' Everywhere that is what he tells us about himself. He put the man and the woman in the Garden and he said, in effect, 'Now keep my commandments, obey my holy law and you will develop, you will grow and you will never die. But if you do not, you will die, you will perish, you will be driven out.' That was a revelation of the holiness of God.

And it is the same with all the prophets. Read it as it is summed up by Habakkuk: 'Thou [God] art of purer eyes than to behold evil' (Hab 1:13). That is the great message of the Old Testament – that God is a holy God, a just, a righteous God. And it was because they did not realise that, that these Children of Israel were so constantly in trouble.

But turn to the New Testament. What about the teaching of the New Testament with respect to God? Take our Lord's own teaching. People say they do not like the God of the Old Testament, but they like 'the God of Jesus'. But what did he say about God? Well, take the Lord's Prayer, the prayer that he taught people to pray. It begins with 'Our Father'! Yes, but do not let the modern person say, 'Ah, God is like a father, is he? Yes, he is like the modern indulgent father who smiles benignly upon you irrespective of what you may or may not do.' No, no! 'Our Father which art in heaven, *hallowed be thy name.*' That is how he teaches us to pray! Not 'Dad'! Not somebody with whom we can be easily familiar, but, 'God, who is in heaven, hallowed be thy name.'

Furthermore, when we have records of our Lord's own prayers, notice how he invariably prayed – he said, 'Holy Father'! Here is our Lord, the incarnation of God's love, and his teaching about God is that he is a holy God, a just God, a righteous God and that he is the very antithesis of sin and evil and all that is wrong. That is our Lord's own teaching.

Go, then, to the teaching of the apostles and you find exactly the same thing. They say, 'God is light, and in him is no darkness at all' (1 Jn 1:5). 'Our God is a consuming fire' (Heb 12:29). All of them are unanimous in their teaching. The teaching of the Bible in the Old Testament and in the New is a great revelation of this august being. Let me say this for the Jews, with all their sinning and all their recalcitrance, they had a fundamental conception of the holiness of God. God had given them his own name. He had said: I am Jehovah! 'I AM THAT I AM' (Ex 3:14). I am that I shall be! I am from eternity to eternity! I am a holy God! They dared not even mention God's name. It was so sacred, so holy, that they referred to 'the Name'. They had been taught this. Look at Moses and the burning bush! He was interested in the phenomenon, and, like a typical modern man, he said to himself, What is this? 'I will now turn aside, and see this great sight' (Ex 3:3). Out came the word: Stand back! 'Put off thy shoes from off thy feet, for the place whereon thou standest is holy ground' (Ex 3:5).

This means that God is not to be examined; he is not a phenomenon for our scientific investigation. God *is*! He is holy and he is fire. God is light. He is justice and righteousness, and I must humble myself before him, take the shoes off my feet for I am on holy ground. I am not the examiner, I am the worshipper. I must be silent, I must listen.

And surely this is something that ought to be obvious to all of us. That is the revelation, and it must be so. The essential attribute of God is glory. Now we cannot define glory, we do not know anything about it, we are so tarnished, so unworthy and polluted. But glory is the absolute in everything: absolute in holiness and righteousness, and justice and love, and mercy and compassion. God is omniscient; he is omnipotent; he is omnipresent. All his attributes are perfect and they are all one in their eternal purity.

> Eternal Light! eternal Light!
> How pure the soul must be,
> When, placed within Thy searching sight,
> It shrinks not, but with calm delight
> Can live and look on Thee.
> *Thomas Binney*

> Immortal, invisible, God only wise,
> In light inaccessible hid from our eyes,
> Most blessed, most glorious, the Ancient of Days,
> Almighty, victorious, Thy great name we praise.
> *Walter Chalmers Smith*

But that description is nothing! It does not define God; he is beyond that. You cannot! All we know is that God is glorious in all his attributes, and it is inconceivable that he should not be holy. If God can mix with sin and evil and vice and the things we are so familiar with, he is no longer God. God is the exact opposite of what I am, in all my smallness, finitude, unworthiness and ugliness. God is the eternal opposite of it all, in all his glory and wonder and perfection, and it is inconceivable that such a God can pretend that he has not seen sin, that he does not hate it, that the whole of his being does not abominate it. God cannot exist with it. So, I say it with reverence, God must do something about sin. The biblical teaching is that he has, and that he will. So this doctrine of the wrath of God is essential, in the first place, to an understanding of God himself.

But, in the second place, this doctrine is absolutely essential to an understanding of human history. And when I say human history I mean the entire known history of civilisation, of the human race, the history that we have available. How is it essential? Well, how do you explain the past history of the world up until this moment? Let me ask the question again: Why is the world as it is? Why the muddle? Why the confusion? Why the suffering, the pain, the agony and the injustice? Why is there so much unhappiness in the world?

Now the Bible has an answer to this and, to me, it is the only adequate answer. It is this: it is not because the world is passing through some painful evolutionary process in the direction of perfection, because there is no evidence that it is. The world is as bad today as it has ever been. No, the answer is that God made a perfect world and put a perfect man and woman in it, and life was meant to be paradise. It was meant to be a holy life, a clean and a pure life, a happy, joyful life.

'So why are things as they are?' you ask.

The Bible has its answer – it is because sin entered, because the man and woman rebelled against God. God told them, in effect, as we have seen, 'Live as I have made you and as I want you to live, and you will have nothing but happiness, but if you do not, you will bring punishment down upon yourselves.'

God warned them – there was no excuse. They were given the terms which were perfectly plain and reasonable. But in their unutterable folly and the arrogance of their pride, they rebelled against God, and God did what he had said he would do. He punished them and he sent them out of Paradise. He said that, henceforth, 'In the sweat of thy face shalt thou eat bread' (Gen 3:19). Not only that, God cursed the earth, we are told; thorns and briers began to arise. Henceforth the life of humanity would be a life of struggle, the seed of the serpent against the seed of the woman, conflict, tension, trouble, wars, calamities, diseases, all these things would come in. This is all a part of the punishment of rebellion and sin. God had warned that it would happen and it did.

And I suggest to you that there is no adequate explanation of the state of the world today but that. There it is, you will find it throughout the Old Testament and it is confirmed many times over in the life of the nations outside the Old Testament history.

God took a man called Abraham, and turned him into a nation. He said, 'I am going to make a people for myself,' and he blessed them and showered his gifts upon them. He told them, 'You have only to live in a manner that will glorify me and I will go on blessing you. If you do not, I will punish you.' But they did not obey him. They rebelled against him, and though they were his own chosen people, he punished them. He raised up enemies against them who conquered them and carried them into captivity.

That is biblical history. It is all a part of the punishment
of sin. As we have seen, you find it in the case of individuals, some of them great men, the greatest men of all. Look
at a man like David. We are told that he was a favourite
with God. And what a mighty man he was, a great king,
a great military leader, a great poet, a great psalmist. And
yet he had to suffer a lot in this world. Why was this?
Because of his sin! David broke the laws of God, he rebelled against God, and punishment came down upon him.
Poor David! He had a tragic sort of life. He started so
well, but look at his end, and it was all because he had not
listened to God; he was bearing the consequences of his
own actions. God punished him, though he was one of
God's choicest servants.

That is the past but it is the same in the present. The
world today is as full of trouble as it has ever been. In
spite of all advances and all our education, the world is in
grievous trouble, and I know of no explanation save that
which is given by the apostle Paul in Romans 1, where he
says three times, 'God gave them up (or over)', as in
Romans 1:28: 'God gave them over to a reprobate mind.'
That is a part of God's punishment. When mankind will
not listen to God nor listen to his appeals, and rejects his
offers, then God begins to punish, and one of the punish-
ments is that he withdraws his restraints. He allows men
and women, as it were, to stew in their own juice. He
says, in effect, 'Very well, you say you can go on without
me, then get on without me.'

And I believe that that is the great, terrible explanation
of this twentieth century of ours, that God is allowing us
to 'get on with it', he is leaving us to ourselves. The
restraints have gone, and all that God does to confine evil
is being held back, and we are witnessing abandonment

and hell let loose. He has handed us over to a reprobate mind.

God had kept on saying through the Old Testament, 'There is no peace . . . to the wicked' (Is 57:21). You may be very learned, but that will not give you peace; you may be very wealthy, but you cannot buy peace. Thank God you cannot! Thank God that in this modern world there are some things that even money cannot do! You cannot buy happiness, you cannot buy tranquillity, you cannot buy the loss of the fear of death. Money is no good, learning is no good – nothing is any good. 'There is no peace, saith my God, to the wicked.' Whether you like it or not, you are in God's world, and God's laws are still being operated. Do what you like, you will never find peace unless you acknowledge God and submit yourself to him.

There is another phrase, as we have seen: 'The way of transgressors is hard' (Prov 13:15). It always has been. You cannot sin with impunity. You will have to pay for it. You will have to pay for it, perhaps, with your health, or in the dulling of your faculties, and in a gradual coarsening of the whole of your outlook. 'The way of transgressors is hard.' It always has been, it still is and it always will be. There is the explanation of the past and the present. What of the future?

Well, according to this great message, things are not going to get any better.

'But,' says somebody, 'I did think at any rate that there was going to be a bit of hope! Yet you say that things are not going to get any better?'

But the Bible tells us, 'Evil men . . . shall wax worse and worse' (2 Tim 3:13), and there will be 'wars and rumours of wars' (Mt 24:6). There may well be political movements and other movements against war, there may well be great efforts to 'ban the bomb' – but you will never stop war.

Why not? Because it is in the human heart. What is the use of getting excited about a tyrant when he marches into another country and annexes it, why your righteous indignation about that, if you excuse an individual man who goes into another man's home and married life and takes his wife? What is the difference in principle? None at all! And that is why the world will never be able to reform itself, or save itself. It has been trying to do it through the running centuries! That is the great story of civilisation. Go back again to Greece. Look at your blueprints of Utopia. Why have we not had it? What is the trouble?

There is only one answer: 'There shall be no peace, saith my God, to the wicked.' Indeed, the biblical message leads to this: that history is working up to a climax. It says that God started the time process, that he is still controlling it, that there is to be an end to the world, and that the world will be judged in righteousness. You will find that throughout the Bible. It is the most awesome thing that we can ever contemplate. But, to me, though it is a terrifying thing, I thank God for it because it tells me that I have got the dignity of responsibility, that I am not a mere machine, that I am not a mere aggregate of biological principles or a mere result of the ductless gland emissions. It tells me that I am a human being and that I am responsible before God; that I have got to appear at a bar of judgement and that I am paid the honour, by God, of having to give an account of my stewardship of the soul that he has given me, and of my conduct and behaviour in this world of time. It is all leading up to an ultimate judgement.

So I am arguing that you do not begin to understand the human story and the history of the world, if you reject this great doctrine of the wrath of God upon sin.

But, lastly, if you reject that doctrine, you will never

understand the grace of God, you will never understand the love of God and you will never understand the gospel. Above all, you will never understand the cross of Christ – never. This is only understood in the light of this biblical teaching concerning God's wrath upon sin, and that is why I am so concerned about this doctrine. By rejecting it, you reject all the most wonderful things in the whole of the gospel.

Look at it like this: if the one thing that we must believe is the love of God, and if, as most people do, you interpret that as meaning that it does not matter what you do, as long as you go to God and say, 'I am sorry,' because he will forgive you, if that is true, then why was the Incarnation ever necessary? If the love of God is the only thing that matters and if it solves all problems, if the whole universe, the whole of humanity, is going to heaven because God is love, why did the Son of God ever come into this world? What was the point? The Children of Israel had been told the message about God as love – 'When my father and my mother forsake me,' says the psalmist, 'then the LORD will take me up' (Ps 27:10), and the prophets are full of this great teaching. I ask, if the love of God alone is the doctrine that we are to believe and if we are to reject the wrath of God, why did the Son of God leave the courts of heaven and be born as a baby? Why did he live in utter poverty? Why did he work with his hands as a carpenter? Why, above all, did he ever die upon that cross? If God is love and that is the only thing, why did he ever allow his Son to go to that death? He could have taken him out of it. Our Lord himself said, in effect, 'If I wanted to escape this I could do it quite easily. I have taken him out of it. Our Lord himself said, in effect, 'If I wanted to escape this I could do it quite easily. I could command twelve legions of angels and they would carry me to heaven' (see Mt 26:53). But no – 'Thus it becometh us to fulfil all righteousness' (Mt 3:15).

But why the cross? And there is only one explanation: it is because of the wrath of God against sin. I say it with reverence, the love of God alone cannot deal with the problem of human sin. It necessitated the Incarnation. And so this leads to the greatest glories of the gospel. Here it is: 'When the fulness of the time was come, God sent forth his Son, made of a woman, made under the law, to redeem them that were under the law' (Gal 4:4–5). Or let me give you again everybody's favourite text: John 3:16, 'For God so loved the world, that he gave his only begotten Son' – why? – 'that whosoever believeth in him should not perish, but have everlasting life.'

There is only one explanation as to why the Son of God ever came into the world, and as to why he ever went to the cross. It is that men and women should not 'perish'! This is the Christian gospel. This is the manifestation of the love of God – that God has sent his Son into the world to save us from the wrath of God upon sin.

Let me summarise that by quoting two verses where the apostle Paul has put it so clearly:

Whom God hath set forth to be a propitiation through faith in his blood, to declare his righteousness for the remission of sins that are past, through the forbearance of God; to declare, I say, at this time his righteousness [God's righteousness]: that he might be just, and the justifier of him which believeth in Jesus (Rom 3:25–26).

What does that mean? It is this. The problem of the forgiveness of sin is the greatest problem that the everlasting God has ever had to face. To make the world was nothing – all he had to say was, 'Let there be light . . . .' A word, a fiat, was enough. But how can men and women be forgiven? Here is the problem, says Paul. How can God be just and yet forgive a sinner? How can God remain holy and utterly removed from sin, and yet forgive people who sin? That is the problem in the mind and the heart of the eternal God.

Love alone cannot solve it because justice and right-eousness insist upon punishment. God's laws must be vindicated, his honour must be vindicated. Sin is an affront to God, an assault upon him and a rebellion against him. What matters is not merely our actions but what they imply in our attitude to God, and for us to sin is to defy the eternal, glorious God who has made every-thing and who owns everything. God's honour, his character and his person must be vindicated. God cannot forgive in a manner that in any way casts any reflection or doubt upon his justice and righteousness.

So that is the problem: How can God remain just, and at the same time justify the ungodly, justify the sinner, justify the rebel – how can he do it? And the answer is, says the apostle Paul, there was only one way and God took it. And if you want to know anything about the love of God it is here that you find it. The love of God to fallen men and women is so great that he has set forth his only Son as 'a propitiation, through faith in his blood'.

'But what does that mean?' asks someone.

It means that though you have sinned and rebelled against God, and though you have made yourself some-thing that is a travesty of human nature, God so loved you that he has put your sins and mine on his only begotten, dearly beloved Son, and the Son took them willingly upon himself. As God considered the problem, the Son, we are told in Scripture, said, 'Here am I; send me' (see Heb 10:7, 9). Someone had to come to bear the punishment. God must be just, and God's justice must punish sin!

Well how can anybody be forgiven? Here is your answer. The sin has been punished in the Son of God, the Lord Jesus Christ. That is why he died! That is why he did not command the twelve legions of angels to save him.

In the Garden of Gethsemane, sweating great drops of blood, he prayed three times and said, 'O my Father, if it be possible, let this cup pass from me: nevertheless not as I will, but as thou wilt' (Mt 26:39). What was he saying? What was this 'cup'? What was this thing from which he shrank? It was not the fear of physical death. The martyrs have not been afraid of that and you make him less than the martyrs if you say that he was merely shrinking from physical pain.

No, it was this: in effect, he turned to his Father and said, 'Is there no other way whereby mankind can be forgiven and saved, except that I take their sins upon me, for that will mean that I will lose your face and that your wrath will be upon me even if only for a second. Is there no other way? If there is not, I will do it.' That is love, that this holy Son of God was made sin for us, and the wrath of God came upon him, and there you hear him crying in agony on the cross, 'My God, my God, why hast thou forsaken me?' (Mt 27:46). The God, into whose face he had looked from eternity, averted his face, and his wrath came down upon him, Jesus Christ, Son of God. And all for the punishment of your sin and mine! That is love! And the result is that God's justice is vindicated and his love is manifested. Justice and love have met together, they have embraced each other. God's holy attributes are all glorified together in the death of the Son of God on the cross.

So you will never know anything about the love of God until you realise God's way of saving us and sparing us from perishing, from bearing the punishment that our sin so richly deserves. In the light of the cross, you have no leg to stand on. It is no use your complaining about the wrath of God, you need never suffer it! God has sent his own Son to save you from it. If you acknowledge your sin and repent and believe on the Lord Jesus Christ, you will never know God's wrath.

So you have no complaint, and if you ever find yourself suffering under God's wrath, you will have nobody to blame but yourself. It was your pride of intellect. You thought you understood God, you thought you could dictate to him as to what he should be, and you said, 'I won't have wrath, I'll only have love' – and so you brought damnation down upon yourself because you insulted God, and you richly deserve it. We all of us deserve the wrath of God!

And no one knows that as well as a Christian. Christians are not what they are because they are good men and women. Christians are vile sinners saved by the grace of God alone. Christians do not glory in themselves and in their good works. Do you know what they do glory in? Let me answer that in the words of a hymn:

> Upon that cross of Jesus,
> Mine eye at times can see
> The very dying form of One
> Who suffered there for me;
> And from my smitten heart, with tears,
> Two wonders I confess –
> The wonders of His glorious love,
> And my own worthlessness.
>
> I take, O Cross, thy shadow,
> For my abiding-place;
> I ask no other sunshine than
> The sunshine of His face;

Content to let the world go by,
To know no gain nor loss –
My sinful self my only shame,
My glory all the cross.

Elizabeth Cecilia Clephane

The day of grace, thank God, is still here. How much longer, I do not know, but does it not seem as if the whole world is preparing for some ultimate cataclysm? It has not come yet, the gate of salvation is still open. If you have seen this truth, acknowledge it to God and enter in through that gate. God will be waiting and willing to pardon all your sins, to apply the blood of Christ to you, to make you a new man or woman and to give you an inheritance among his children in the glory everlasting.